T0354262

EVIDENCE BASED TEACHING in SECONDARY SCHOOLS

Sara Miller McCune founded SAGE Publishing in 1965 to support the dissemination of usable knowledge and educate a global community. SAGE publishes more than 1000 journals and over 800 new books each year, spanning a wide range of subject areas. Our growing selection of library products includes archives, data, case studies and video. SAGE remains majority owned by our founder and after her lifetime will become owned by a charitable trust that secures the company's continued independence.

Los Angeles | London | New Delhi | Singapore | Washington DC | Melbourne

EVIDENCE BASED TEACHING in SECONDARY SCHOOLS

JONATHAN GLAZZARD
AND SAMUEL STONES

Learning Matters
A SAGE Publishing Company
1 Oliver's Yard
55 City Road
London EC1Y 1SP

SAGE Publications Inc.
2455 Teller Road
Thousand Oaks, California 91320

SAGE Publications India Pvt Ltd
B 1/I 1 Mohan Cooperative Industrial Area
Mathura Road
New Delhi 110 044

SAGE Publications Asia-Pacific Pte Ltd
3 Church Street
#10-04 Samsung Hub
Singapore 049483

© 2022 Jonathan Glazzard and Samuel Stones

First published in 2022

Apart from any fair dealing for the purposes of
research, private study, or criticism or review, as
permitted under the Copyright, Designs and Patents
Act, 1988, this publication may not be reproduced,
stored or transmitted in any form, or by any means,
without the prior permission in writing of the publisher,
or in the case of reprographic reproduction, in
accordance with the terms of licences issued by the
Copyright Licensing Agency. Enquiries concerning
reproduction outside those terms should be sent to
the publisher.

Editor: Amy Thornton
Senior project editor: Chris Marke
Project management: River Editorial
Cover design: Wendy Scott
Typeset by: C&M Digitals (P) Ltd, Chennai, India
Printed in the UK

Library of Congress Control Number: 2021947638

British Library Cataloguing in Publication Data

A catalogue record for this book is available from the
British Library

ISBN 978-1-5297-5577-0
ISBN 978-1-5297-5576-3 (pbk)

At SAGE we take sustainability seriously. Most of our products are printed in the UK using responsibly sourced
papers and boards. When we print overseas we ensure sustainable papers are used as measured by the
PREPS grading system. We undertake an annual audit to monitor our sustainability.

CONTENTS

ABOUT THE AUTHORS

Jonathan Glazzard is Professor of Teacher Education and Head of Department at Edge Hill University. He leads one of the largest departments of primary initial teacher education in the UK. His research focuses on mental health, inclusion, special educational needs and disabilities. Jonathan has worked in four universities and he worked as a primary school teacher between 1995–2005.

Samuel Stones is an Associate Researcher in the Carnegie School of Education at Leeds Beckett University. His research outputs are linked with the Centre for LGBTQ+ Inclusion in Education and the Carnegie Centre of Excellence for Mental Health in Schools. Samuel's research explores the experiences of teachers who identify as lesbian, gay, bisexual and transgender, with specific emphasis on the impact of sexual orientation on teacher identity and mental health. He also works with initial teacher training students in university and school contexts and is an Associate Leader of maths, computing, economics and business at a secondary school and sixth form college in North Yorkshire.

iNTRODUCTioN

The *Initial Teacher Training (ITT) Market Review Report* that was published in July 2021 reported the following:

> *Ofsted ... found that too often, curriculums were underpinned by outdated or discredited theories of education and not well enough informed by the most pertinent research and concluded that 'the ITE sector must now develop stronger and more ambitious ITE curriculums. This means developing curriculums that are better designed around subject and phase, more integrated across the partnership, and more informed by up-to-date and pertinent research'.*

(p8)

In response, this book provides trainee teachers and teachers with a synthesis of some of the latest research findings and current thinking in relation to education. It is important that all teachers understand the evidence base which underpins specific pedagogical approaches. Research evidence highlights specific approaches which are more likely to be successful in producing gains in learning. In this respect, we have focused on the role of application of cognitive science and neuroscience to educational practice. We have also included sections on memory, cognitive load, interleaving, and distributed and retrieval practice. Many schools are now adopting some of these pedagogical approaches, although there is still a need for more evidence on their effectiveness. Despite the research gaps on the application of cognitive science in education, we believe that these approaches are worth knowing and worth implementing. We have also devoted a whole chapter to education myths. We have debunked some of the key myths and we have highlighted approaches that are more likely to be effective.

Many teachers have not received a strong grounding in psychology, unless of course they have studied for an undergraduate or postgraduate qualification in psychology. Even then, the psychology content may not have been applied to education. The *ITT Core Content Framework* (CCF) (2019a) now sets out the minimum content that all ITT/ITE providers should embed within their teacher education programmes. There is a strong psychological component in this framework and therefore new teachers should now enter the profession with a good level of knowledge of psychology and its application to education. It is refreshing that there is a greater emphasis now within initial teacher training and within the *Early Career Framework* (ECF) (2019b) on how children learn. We believe that all teachers need this knowledge.

However, we wish to emphasise that dated educational theories are not necessarily bad theories. Although we believe that cognition plays a critical role in learning, we do not dismiss the role of sociocultural theory in children's learning and development. Learning is influenced by teachers, peers, families, cultures and communities and we believe that the work of Vygotsky is particularly important in helping teachers to understand the role of social and cultural factors in learning and specifically the role of the teacher.

The progressivist–traditionalist divide is not helpful. Both paradigms have something to offer to education. The evidence is clear that students benefit from direct teaching, particularly when subject content is modelled and explained and introduced in small steps with opportunities for guided and independent practice after each step. The evidence supports this approach, particularly for novice learners. Effective curriculum design, through careful sequencing of curriculum content, supports students to make connections between new knowledge and existing knowledge. However, we do believe that student-centred approaches, through problem-solving or collaborative group work, have a role to play in learning. Although we do not focus on these specifically in this book, students do need to be able to work in teams, they do need to be able to negotiate conflict and they do need to develop solutions to solving problems. They need to be given opportunities to research information and present their research. Without these skills, students will not be independent learners and they will not be well-prepared for higher education or the workplace. Tom Sherrington (2019a) does not dismiss these approaches but argues that they should not be used as vehicles for students to make discoveries. The teacher needs to teach the substantive subject knowledge content first before students can apply this to solving problems.

Each chapter provides a synthesis of the key research findings. We have also provided useful examples of classroom practice and key take-aways in all chapters.

1
EDUCATIONAL DISADVANTAGE AND INCLUSION

TEACHERS' STANDARDS

This chapter addresses TS1, which requires teachers to set goals that stretch and challenge pupils of all backgrounds, abilities and dispositions.

IN THIS CHAPTER

This chapter addresses the impact of educational disadvantage on achievement. The needs of specific groups of students are considered, along with the role of school leaders in addressing issues of inclusion. Disadvantage, either because of poverty or minority status, can impact significantly on the life chances of young people. We argue that school leaders and teachers should have high expectations of all students and support them in raising their aspirations. We also outline the role of the curriculum as a leveller through providing students with cultural capital.

KEY POLICY DOCUMENTATION

The *ITT Core Content Framework* states that trainees must learn that:

> *High-quality teaching has a long-term positive effect on pupils' life chances, particularly for children from disadvantaged backgrounds.*

(DfE, 2019a, p9)

DISADVANTAGE

This chapter focuses on the role of poverty in creating educational disadvantage. However, it also addresses broader aspects of inclusion, specifically LGBTQ+ inclusion in secondary schools. Poverty impacts detrimentally on educational and life outcomes. Schools cannot compensate for the effects of disadvantage, but they can reduce the effects. The National

Education Union states that 'our education system does not have to mirror the society and economy within which it is situated' (2021, p8). This is a critical point to reflect upon.

Schools can play a significant role in reducing the attainment gap between disadvantaged students and their non-disadvantaged peers by providing access to a broad and rich curriculum that provides students with powerful knowledge. Schools can create opportunities for students by providing them with experiences that they would otherwise not get. Disadvantaged students may have less cultural capital than their non-disadvantaged peers. The relationship between cultural capital and good life outcomes is clear – cultural capital provides access to social, cultural and economic opportunities and increases social mobility. By developing a school curriculum which embeds cultural capital, the curriculum then serves as a leveller by minimising the effects of disadvantage and creating equality of opportunity. The school curriculum should provide access to knowledge that takes them beyond their immediate experiences. The sociologist Michael Young offers several definitions of powerful knowledge:

> *Powerful knowledge refers to what the knowledge can do or what intellectual power it gives to those who have access to it. Powerful knowledge provides more reliable explanations and new ways of thinking about the world and … can provide learners with a language for engaging in political, moral, and other kinds of debates.*

> (Young, 2008, p14)

> *'Powerful knowledge' is powerful because it provides the best understanding of the natural and social worlds that we have and helps us go beyond our individual experiences.*

> (Young, 2013, p196)

> *Knowledge is 'powerful' if it predicts, if it explains, if it enables you to envisage alternatives.*

> (Young, 2014, p74)

Back in 2013, Michael Gove, then Secretary of State, stated that 'The acquisition of cultural capital – the acquisition of knowledge – is the key to social mobility'. Cultural capital prepares students well to compete economically in a global society.

However, there is a fine balancing act to be done. The curriculum should develop students' knowledge of places and cultures beyond their immediate locality. It should extend their vocabularies and provide students with opportunities to learn specialist and deep knowledge. Paragraph 163 of the *School Inspection Handbook* (Ofsted, 2019) defines this as 'the essential knowledge that pupils need to be educated citizens, introducing them to the *best that has been thought and said* and helping to engender an appreciation of human creativity and achievement' [our emphasis]. It should confront prejudices head on and provide students with rich experiences that extend their cultural and linguistic knowledge. At the same time, the curriculum should reflect students' backgrounds and experiences so that students know that their backgrounds are recognised, valued and respected. Research demonstrates that many working-class students experience a sense of powerlessness and educational worthlessness as well as feeling that they are not really valued and respected within education (Reay, 2017). A culturally responsive pedagogy is premised on the idea that valuing the cultural worlds of students is central to learning. Teachers should understand the socio-cultural worlds of their students, listen to them, value them and incorporate their cultural identities and histories within the curriculum. A culturally responsive pedagogy nourishes them intellectually, socially, emotionally and politically, and prepares them for a contemporary multicultural and multiracial world (Lucas and Villegas, 2013; Nieto, 2000; Sleeter, 2011). A culturally responsive pedagogy also enhances their cognitive development and self-esteem, enables students to express their own cultural identities and be proud of them.

KEY RESEARCH

The National Education Union (NEU) has produced a synthesis of key research. This is summarised below.

- Poverty is the strongest statistical predictor of how well a child will achieve at school.

- By Year 6, pupils living in poverty are often over nine months behind their peers in reading, writing and mathematics.

- The attainment gap widens for pupils throughout secondary school. Students eligible for free school meals are half as likely to achieve a good pass at GCSE in English and mathematics in comparison to other students.

- Students living in poverty are four times more likely to be permanently excluded from school than their peers.

- Even with the same qualifications, disadvantaged students are 50 per cent more likely to be Not in Education, Employment or Training (NEET) after leaving school.

- Single parents are more likely to experience poverty than those families with both parents.

- People from Black and Ethnic Minority groups are also more likely to live in poverty.

(NEU, 2021)

RACE AND ETHNICITY

Race and ethnicity impact on students' experience of education in a way that can perpetuate inequalities and, in some cases, create poverty. An unrepresentative curriculum and racism contribute to the systemic exclusion of young black, Asian and minority ethnic (BAME) people. BAME students are not only disadvantaged due to poverty, they are also disadvantaged by the curriculum and exposure to minority stress (Meyer, 2003). Specific groups of BAME students are more likely to underachieve, resulting in poor long-term outcomes. This prevents them from escaping the cycle of poverty. Some key facts are summarised below.

- Child poverty rates are 60 and 54 per cent for children from Bangladeshi and Pakistani families, respectively.
- Black and Ethnic Minority people are more likely to be in low-paid employment.
- Black and Ethnic Minority households are more likely to include larger families.

(NEU, 2021)

STUDENTS WITH SPECIAL EDUCATIONAL NEEDS OR DISABILITY (SEND)

Children and young people with SEND are more likely to be bullied, may find it harder to make friends and are more likely to be permanently excluded. Long-term outcomes are poor. Far too many do not achieve good qualifications or gain entry to employment, training, further and higher education. This traps them in a cycle of poverty. Some key facts are outlined below.

- In the UK, 31 per cent of households with a disabled family member were living in poverty compared to 19 per cent without.
- Forty per cent of families where there is a disabled child are living in poverty.

(NEU, 2021)

REFUGEES AND MIGRANT STUDENTS

Refugees, migrants and those with no recourse to public funds (NRPF) are often trapped in a cycle of poverty. Children and young people who are refugees or migrants and whose families have no recourse to public funds experience disruption to their education. They often have inadequate and insecure housing, as well as lack of knowledge of the English education system. Evidence also suggests that many migrant children take on additional caring responsibilities which teachers do not always know about.

LGBTQ+ STUDENTS

Students who are lesbian, gay, bisexual, trans or queer experience educational disadvantage. This is because they are more likely than non-LGBTQ+ students to experience poor mental health due to exposure to bullying, prejudice and discrimination. Key statistics are presented below.

- Nearly half of lesbian, gay, bi and trans students (45 per cent), including 64 per cent of trans students, are bullied for being LGBT at school.

- Fifty-two per cent hear homophobic language 'frequently' or 'often' at school.

- Eighty-six per cent regularly hear phrases such as 'that's so gay' or 'you're so gay' in school.

- Nearly one in ten trans students (9 per cent) are subjected to death threats at school.

- Eighty-four per cent of trans young people have self-harmed.

- For lesbian, gay and bi young people who aren't trans, 61 per cent have self-harmed.

- Forty-five per cent of trans students have attempted to take their own life. For lesbian, gay and bi young people who aren't trans, 22 per cent have attempted to take their own life.

(Bradlow et al., 2017, p6)

Students must learn about LGBTQ+ content as part of relationships and sex education in secondary schools. It is not adequate for schools to only address prejudice-based bullying. The Equality Act 2010 places a duty on schools to promote good relations between those with and without protected characteristics. Sexual orientation, race, gender reassignment and disability are examples of protected characteristics. Schools cannot meet their statutory duties if different identities are not visible in the curriculum and if students are not taught to respect those with different identities. Social justice and inclusion should be at the heart of school improvement. Gorard (2010, p62) argues that 'schools, in their structure and organisation, can do more than simply reflect the society we have; they can try to be the precursor of the kind of society that we wish to have'. The best way of addressing this is to provide students with a curriculum that promotes social justice.

INTERSECTIONALITY

This chapter has addressed different categories of identities. It is important to emphasise that students may have intersecting identities. A student may have SEND, be LGBTQ+ and they may be living in poverty. This is only one example, but it serves to illustrate that young people may be exposed to multiple forms of disadvantage. This can impact negatively on attainment, mental health and long-term outcomes.

WHOLE SCHOOL APPROACH TO INCLUSION

This chapter has deliberately not addressed the overwhelming amount of research and literature on inclusion. Instead, we have pinpointed the key issues and presented some key data. This section examines more practically what schools can do to address disadvantage. We propose a model of the whole school approach to inclusion as shown in Figure 1.1.

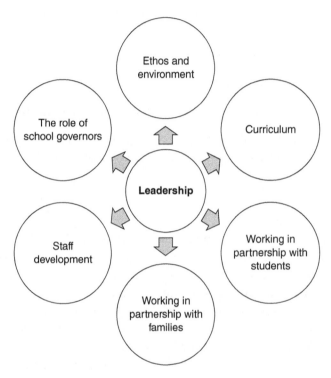

Figure 1.1 Whole school approach to inclusion

Each of the aspects of the model will now be addressed.

LEADERSHIP

The senior leadership team play a critical role in championing inclusion. The starting point is for leadership teams to place social justice and inclusion at the heart of school improvement. One way of addressing this is for leaders to be clear that the intent of the curriculum is underpinned by an unrelenting commitment to social justice. This can be addressed through embedding poverty, race, disability, sexual orientation and gender into the curriculum. The National Curriculum does not directly address these themes. Students' misconceptions about poverty and disadvantage need to be addressed. Students need to be provided with a curriculum that not only promotes cultural capital but a curriculum that addresses prejudice and discrimination directly in relation to all these themes. Students need to be provided with a broad and rich curriculum which challenges them academically and shapes and transforms their values in relation to equality. Providing students with a broad and rich curriculum, in combination with a broad co-curriculum, will mitigate some of the effects of disadvantage. Fundamentally, students from all social backgrounds and with a diverse range of identities need their identities to be visible in the curriculum. In addition, the curriculum should provide students with the knowledge that they need and the aspirations to achieve great things regardless of their social backgrounds. It should empower them to be proud of their backgrounds and their identities.

ETHOS AND ENVIRONMENT

The ethos and environment are critical aspects of the whole school approach. School leaders should work hard to create a positive ethos so that students feel safe. Some children who are experiencing disadvantage or have experienced prejudice, bullying and discrimination do not feel safe. Schools should be a place of safety and sanctuary for all students so that they can thrive. Strong messages which promote inclusion, social justice, effort and aspiration should be embedded throughout the physical environment of the school. This will support students to experience a sense of belonging and instil a determination to achieve.

CURRICULUM

The leadership team should empower teachers to educate students about poverty, disadvantage, prejudice and diversity. The curriculum should be decolonised, and subject teachers need to ensure that they are not just covering the achievements of white, cisgender, middle-class, middle-aged males. Providing a curriculum for social justice means that teachers should be prepared to teach content that is challenging. Issues of social disadvantage and other forms of disadvantage, for example, systemic racism, exploitation and homophobia, should be addressed as the backbone of the curriculum and interwoven into subjects. Students need to be taught explicitly about the harmful effects of discrimination, both on individuals and on society. They should be taught to critically debate political decisions that have directly been responsible for creating or sustaining disadvantage.

WORKING IN PARTNERSHIP WITH STUDENTS

Students should be empowered to be leaders of social justice. Developing the role of the 'social justice' champion is one way of working with students to address disadvantage, equality and social justice. This role could be developed in partnership with students. This initiative assigns students with agency.

WORKiNG iN PARTNERSHiP WiTH FAMiLiES

In relation to disadvantage, schools should consider the following questions:

- How much notice do families get about events and activities in school that require resources or money?

- Who should families speak to at school if they are struggling with school-related costs?

- How do families know what help and support might be available?

Recent initiatives during the global pandemic have demonstrated the immense capacities of schools to support communities to address the effects of disadvantage. School leaders might wish to consider what initiatives might be offered to parents in areas of social disadvantage to develop their functional skills and support their wellbeing.

STAFF DEVELOPMENT

Staff may benefit from specific training to address disadvantage. Key questions for teachers to consider are:

- How do you know which families are finding things difficult financially?

- How does poverty impact on the lives of children and families in your school?

- How do you ensure that differences in family finances aren't highlighted in the classroom?

- How do you address students' misconceptions about poverty?

- How do you address prejudice and discrimination when you witness it?

- How might you build cultural capital in your subject curriculum so that all students can access opportunities in the future?

- How might you address questions of inclusion and social justice in your subject curriculum?

THE ROLE OF GOVERNORS

Governors should receive specific training in social disadvantage and other forms of educational disadvantage (for example, racism). Without this training, they cannot effectively monitor the work that the school is undertaking in this area. School leaders should consider appointing a specific governor to take responsibility for disadvantage.

iN THE CLASSROOM

Provide students with statement cards that address facts and myths about poverty. Examples can include:

People are poor because they are lazy and don't want to work.

Poverty is relative to the contexts in different countries.

Ask them to sort the statements into myths and facts and to discuss the reasons for their choices.

TAKE 5

- The school curriculum should directly address issues of social justice.

- School environments and teaching resources should reflect the diverse identities that are represented in the school.

- The curriculum must embed opportunities for developing cultural capital.

- Working in partnership with students to address matters of social justice provides them with agency, leadership skills and empowerment.

- Staff training and development is crucial so that teachers are confident to address matters of social justice.

SUMMARY

The secondary school curriculum should address matters of social justice. Poverty, race, disability, sexuality and gender should be embedded into the curriculum. The purpose of this is to transform students' attitudes, values and beliefs about disadvantage and minority status. Students need to understand how people's attitudes towards minorities have changed over time, about the treatment of specific groups of people in the past and about the prejudice and discrimination that are still evident in contemporary society. Education should play a powerful role in promoting social justice through transforming the attitudes and values of future generations.

2
HOW CHILDREN LEARN

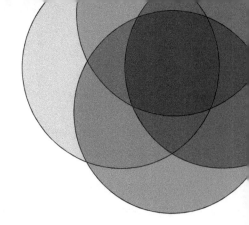

TEACHERS' STANDARDS

This chapter addresses elements of TS2, which focuses on promoting good progress and outcomes for learners.

┌─ IN THIS CHAPTER ───

This chapter addresses the latest thinking about how children learn. The role of the working and long-term memory is highlighted and the contribution of neuroscience to children's learning is also addressed. Some applications of cognitive science are addressed, including the role of spaced or distributed practice and retrieval. These approaches will also be discussed in subsequent chapters.

KEY POLICY DOCUMENTATION

The *ITT Core Content Framework* states that trainees must learn that:

- working memory is where information that is being actively processed is held, but its capacity is limited and can be overloaded;

- long-term memory can be considered as a store of knowledge that changes as pupils learn by integrating new ideas with existing knowledge.

(DfE, 2019a, p11)

KEY RESEARCH

The evidence from research (Darling-Hammond et al., 2020) has demonstrated that:

- students' learning and development is shaped by a combination of environmental factors and learning opportunities both inside and outside schools;

- learning involves physical, psychological, social and emotional processes. These influence one another in that the interactions between these processes can enable or restrict learning;

- the brain and intelligence are malleable and can be changed by environmental influences, including exposure to high-quality teaching;

- our experiences activate neural pathways that enable new ways of thinking and new skills to develop;

- emotions and social contexts shape neural connections which contribute to attention, concentration and memory as well as knowledge transfer and application. Research has demonstrated that chronic stress due to trauma affects cognition and working memory;

- differentiated instruction enables optimum brain growth.

WHAT DO WE KNOW ABOUT BRAIN DEVELOPMENT?

Research demonstrates that:

> *Experience is a 'stressor' to brain growth – throughout life, interpersonal experiences and relational connections activate neural pathways, generating energy flow through electrical impulses that strengthen connectivity.*

> (Cantor et al., 2019, p311)

A combination of both genetic factors and early experiences shape neuronal connections which develop neural circuits. These enable increasingly complex mental activities to occur (Moore, 2015; Slavich and Cole, 2013). As these circuits become increasingly stable, they contribute to the development of complex thoughts, skills and behaviours in individuals (Cantor et al., 2019). Environmental and interpersonal experiences influence brain growth throughout childhood and well into adulthood. It has been demonstrated that 'genes act as followers, not prime movers, in developmental processes' (Cantor et al., 2019, p309). It has also been demonstrated that positive, nurturing relationships are essential to brain development. These relationships build strong brain architecture (Cantor et al., 2019). We know that students' development is shaped by micro-ecological contexts (i.e. families, peers, schools and communities) as well as macro-ecological contexts (i.e. economic and cultural systems).

The brain is characterised by plasticity rather than stability. Its structure is influenced not just by genetics but by the micro and macro contexts within which individuals are situated.

Physical, psychological, social and emotional processes also influence brain structure. Emotions can have powerful effects on developmental pathways (Cantor et al., 2019). The implications of this are significant because the research demonstrates that an individual's experiences can shape the development of neural pathways which facilitate mental processes. Thus, exposure to high-quality teaching can change the structure of the brain by activating new neural pathways.

PROMOTiNG A GROWTH MiNDSET: BRAiN DEVELOPMENT

Research demonstrates that the brain can physically change and that this can occur well into adulthood (Abiola and Dhindsa, 2012). Research undertaken by Maguire et al. (2006) examined the physical changes in the brains of individuals undertaking training to become London taxi drivers. The research demonstrated that following the training, there was a significant growth in the hippocampus, the area of the brain that processes spatial information (Maguire et al., 2006). Research that demonstrates the plasticity of the brain supports the belief that intellectual ability can be enhanced and developed through learning (Sternberg, 2005). It therefore supports the idea of a 'growth mindset' (Dweck, 1999). People with growth mindsets believe that intelligence can grow and be developed through effort. In contrast, those with fixed mindsets view intelligence as a static trait and not something that can be developed.

Dweck (2007, 2009) argued that mindsets play a critical role in the motivation and achievement of learners. Learners with a fixed mindset can easily give up when learning becomes too challenging. Conversely, learners with a growth mindset embrace learning opportunities that provide challenge, even where failure is a very real possibility (Dweck, 2007). Although two individuals with differing mindsets can start out achieving similar levels academically, research suggests that over time, the individual with the growth mindset will begin to outperform the individual with the fixed mindset (Dweck, 2009). Research demonstrates that 'at every socioeconomic level, those who hold more of a growth mindset consistently outperform those who do not' (Claro et al., 2016, p4).

Fixed-ability thinking can encourage inequality (Boaler, 2013) because individuals with fixed mindsets may lack motivation and resilience and may not be prepared to invest effort into developing their brain. In the worst cases, these individuals give up on learning and develop 'learned helplessness'.

The attitudes of teachers towards intelligence and school culture play an important role in how students view themselves. The use of ability groupings in schools promotes the idea of a fixed mindset (Boaler, 2013). Boaler (2013) has argued that ability groupings transmit to students the view that some students are not capable of completing more challenging tasks, thus suggesting that intelligence is static. Static groups are common in schools; the opportunity to change groups is limited (Davies et al., 2003; Dixon, 2002) and research suggests that most students remain in the same ability group for the duration of their school career (Ollerton, 2001). This promotes the idea of a fixed mindset that is transmitted to students.

Dweck (2010) suggests that the culture and learning approaches within schools could help students to change their approach to learning and encourage the development of growth mindset beliefs. A shift in culture may require teachers to re-frame their perceptions of intelligence and for schools to review the use of fixed-ability groups.

DiSTRiBUTED PRACTiCE

According to Sweller et al. (2011), 'if nothing in the long-term memory has been altered, nothing has been learned'. Research suggests that an effective approach to curriculum planning is to repeat practice over time, as this leads to better long-term retention of knowledge (Rawson and Kintsch, 2005). This is known as spaced or distributed practice. Reviewing previous learning leads to much greater long-term retention if subject content is spread out, with gaps in between to allow students to forget the content (Coe et al., 2014). This 'is one of the most general and robust effects from across the entire history of experimental research on learning and memory' (Bjork and Bjork, 2011, p59). Many students benefit from repeated exposure to subject content, particularly when content is spaced out and revisited rather than taught in a single block and never revisited.

MEMORY

'Memory is the term given to the structures and processes involved in the storage and subsequent retrieval of information' (McLeod, 2013). The development of memory is critical to learning. There are two *main* types of memory: the working memory and the long-term memory. The working memory holds a limited amount of information which is used to execute cognitive tasks. It enables individuals to hold multiple pieces of information which are used to complete a variety of daily tasks. In contrast, the long-term memory stores information indefinitely, including information which is not being used in the working memory. Repetition is required to 'fix' information in the long-term memory, but once it is stored in the long-term memory, it can remain there for a significant time.

WORKiNG MEMORY: THE WORKiNG MEMORY MODEL (BADDELEY AND HiTCH, 1974)

The working memory is the part of the memory that enables us to complete tasks. Baddeley and Hitch proposed a model of working memory in 1974, in an attempt to describe a more accurate model of short-term memory. The model of Baddeley and Hitch is composed of three main components: the 'central executive', which acts as the main system and controls the flow of information from and to its 'slave-systems', the 'phonological loop' and the 'visuospatial sketch pad'. The slave systems are short-term storage systems. Each is dedicated to a content domain (verbal and visuospatial, respectively).

Thus, the components of working memory include:

- the central executive: this drives the working memory and the subsystems of working memory, the phonological loop and the visuospatial sketch pad. It also deals with cognitive tasks;

- the visuospatial sketch pad: this stores and processes information in a visual or spatial form and is therefore essential for navigation. This is a slave system of the central executive;

- the phonological loop: this is part of working memory that deals with spoken and written material. This is a slave system of the central executive;

- the episodic buffer: this is a temporary storage system that combines information from the phonological loop and the visuospatial sketch pad. It also communicates with the long-term memory.

The model is represented visually in Figure 2.1.

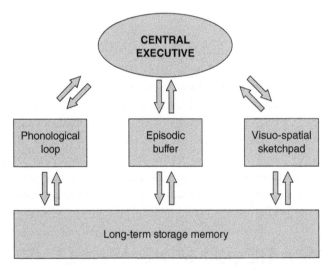

Figure 2.1 *The components of the working memory*

(source: Baddeley and Hitch, 1974)

The working memory is an active, temporary memory system which enables us to store information while we are completing a task. It holds multiple pieces of information, but its capacity is limited to approximately seven pieces of information.

THE PHONOLOGICAL LOOP

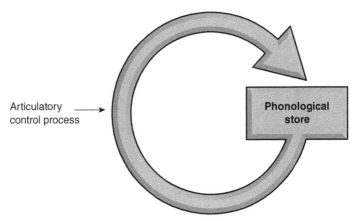

Figure 2.2   The phonological loop

The phonological loop (see Figure 2.2) is a component of the working memory model that processes auditory information. It maintains information that is presented as an auditory code. It is subdivided into the phonological store, which holds the information that we hear, and the articulatory process, which enables us to rehearse words that are in the phonological store. Spoken information enters the phonological store directly. Written information must be converted into sound before it can enter the phonological store. The articulatory control process converts written information such as words and numbers into an articulatory code and transfers them to the phonological store. The process operates as a loop because if we keep repeating auditory information, the information is retained in the working memory. If you are trying to memorise your mobile phone number, the process of repeating it transfers the number into the phonological store and into the working memory.

VISUOSPATIAL SKETCH PAD

The visuospatial sketch pad enables us to store visual and spatial information. It is subdivided into a visual store and a spatial store which together support visual and spatial processing. It is the part of the working memory that is responsible for spatial awareness and navigation. If you are trying to remember the route to a particular building on a university campus, this is the part of the memory that you are activating. If you are trying to find your car in a large car park, you are processing this task visually (looking for the colour of your car) but also spatially (remembering the route to your car). The visuospatial sketch pad is an active component of the working memory.

EPISODIC BUFFER

The episodic buffer was added later to the model by Baddeley (2000). It is a temporary store which combines information from the phonological loop, the visuospatial sketch pad and the long-term memory. It enables information from these stores to be held temporarily and combines the information under the control of the central executive. If you are completing a task which combines visual, spatial and auditory information, you are drawing on both of the slave systems of the working memory, that is the phonological loop and the visuospatial sketch pad.

KEY FACTS ABOUT THE WORKING MEMORY

- The phonological loop allows us to remember auditory information through the process of repetition (for example, learning a telephone number by repeating it).

- Information that enters the phonological loop as an auditory code is transferred into the phonological store.

- Information that enters the phonological loop as a visual code (for example, a written word) has to be converted to an auditory code before it can enter the phonological store.

- The visuospatial sketch pad allows us to store visual and spatial information.

- Both the phonological loop and the visuospatial sketch pad are slave systems of the central executive.

- Tasks which interfere with each other cause cognitive overload. This happens when tasks use the same component of the working memory. An example of this is when we try to learn a set of letters while counting backwards in threes from 100. Both tasks require the phonological loop and therefore interfere with each other.

- The working memory can cope with more than one task provided that different components of the working memory are used, for example, completing an auditory task at the same time as completing a task which requires the retrieval of visual or spatial information from the sketch pad. The episodic buffer will combine the information from both slave systems to enable this task to be completed.

- Serial processing is when a component of the working memory completes one task before completing another.

- Parallel processing is when both slave systems (i.e. the phonological loop and the visuospatial sketch pad) complete tasks at the same time.

2 How children learn

LONG-TERM MEMORY

We can store information in the long-term memory for a few minutes, long periods of time or sometimes even for a lifetime. It has unlimited capacity. However, our capacity to retrieve information influences whether we can recall the information that the long-term memory holds. It includes:

- *semantic memory*: this is a part of the long-term memory responsible for storing information about the world. This includes knowledge about the meaning of words, as well as general knowledge;

- *episodic memory*: this is a part of the long-term memory responsible for storing information about events (i.e. episodes) that we have experienced in our lives;

- *procedural memory*: this is the aspect of our memory that helps us to remember how to do things, for example, how to fasten a knot in a tie or how to tie our shoelaces.

INFORMATION PROCESSING

Memory covers three important aspects of information processing:

- memory encoding;

- memory storage;

- memory retrieval.

MEMORY ENCODING

When information comes into our memory system through our senses, it needs to be changed into a form that the system can cope with so that it can be stored. This process is known as encoding. For example, a word which is seen (in a book) may be stored if it is changed (encoded) into a sound or a meaning (i.e. semantic processing).

For example, students can remember a word that they have read in a book (visual processing) by changing the word into the sound (auditory processing). They may code the word in their memory by sound. In addition, students may attach a meaning to the word (semantic processing). The memory therefore uses the following types of coding when information comes into the memory:

- visual;

- acoustic;

- semantic.

Evidence suggests that acoustic coding is the principle coding system in the short-term memory (McLeod, 2013). We remember information by rehearsing the information verbally. Think back to when you were at school, and you had to remember the first twenty elements in the periodic table in chemistry. It is likely that you repeated them verbally. They are converted from visual information to auditory information in the short-term memory. Think about how you remember a telephone number. It is likely that you convert it from visual information to auditory information by repeating it several times. The telephone number then goes into your memory as an acoustic code rather than a visual code. Research suggests that the principle encoding system in long-term memory appears to be semantic coding (by meaning) (McLeod, 2013). We attach meanings to the information that enter the long-term memory. However, information in the long-term memory can also be coded acoustically and visually.

MEMORY STORAGE

Memory storage concerns the nature of memory stores, that is where the information is stored, how long the memory lasts for (duration), how much can be stored at any time (capacity) and what kind of information is held (McLeod, 2013).

Research suggests that most adults can store between five and nine items in their short-term memory (McLeod, 2013). Miller (1956) proposed that individuals were capable of storing seven items of information (or memory 'slots') in the short-term memory. However, it is possible to group pieces of information together so that several pieces of information can fit into each slot, which then increases the amount of information that can be stored in the short-term memory. Information can only be stored in the short-term memory for a limited amount of time.

The short-term memory stores small amounts of information for short periods of time with relatively little processing; it is a single store without any subsystems. In contrast, working memory is not a unitary store; it can hold multiple pieces of information.

MEMORY RETRIEVAL

This is the process of retrieving information from storage. If we cannot remember something, it may be because we are unable to retrieve it from the memory. If information is stored sequentially, then this process aids retrieval. For this reason, it is important to consider carefully how to sequence subject-specific content in teaching. If teachers spend time thinking about how to sequence subject-specific knowledge, concepts and skills, this will mean that information can be stored sequentially in the memory. This will support memory retrieval.

COGNITIVE LOAD

Cognitive load theory addresses techniques for managing working memory load in order to enable learners to process complex cognitive tasks (Paas et al., 2003). The aim is to reduce the load on the working memory so that it can function more efficiently. If a single slave system of the working memory is attempting to complete two tasks at the same time, the tasks will conflict with each other, resulting in cognitive load. Each slave system can complete a task in parallel at the same time and the tasks will not conflict because each task is being completed using a separate component of the working memory. Teachers can reduce the load on the working memory by breaking down or 'chunking' information in manageable ways and by connecting new learning to previous learning. Research has also found that cognitive load in the classroom is exacerbated by adverse experiences that students are exposed to (Darling-Hammond et al., 2020) because they are actively processing those experiences as well as processing tasks in the classroom.

SCHEMAS

One of the ways through which the brain stores information is through the development of schemas. Schemas are mental structures or frameworks for representing some aspect of the world, including knowledge. Organising knowledge into schemas facilitates its retrieval from the long-term memory. Schemas are mental structures that are stored in the long-term memory. Developing accurate schemas is important to help students understand how subject-specific content is connected, but it also ensures that information can be easily retrieved from the long-term memory. Think of it as being like a filing cabinet or the folders of information on a computer. Piaget (1896–1980) articulated how new learning occurs using schemas. He used the term 'assimilation' when new information is added to current schemas. When new information 'slots into place' with previously stored information, the schema works and there is a state of 'equilibrium'. However, 'disequilibrium' occurs when new information cannot be fitted into existing schemas. This causes the student to experience what Piaget referred to as 'cognitive dissonance'. This is where schemas are forced to change to 'accommodate' new information. This happens when the existing knowledge does not slot easily into an existing schema and the schema needs to be modified to accommodate the new information.

A student may develop a schema about the structure of an atom. They learn that an atom is circular, that it has a central nucleus, protons, neutrons and electrons that orbit the nucleus. However, when the student learns chemistry at an advanced level, the schema no longer works and needs to be changed because they learn that atomic structure is more complex. The process of reframing a schema can be challenging, but this is when learning occurs. It is the process through which new knowledge is accommodated with existing knowledge to return to a state of equilibrium.

NEUROSCIENCE AND EDUCATION

In recent years, there has been increased interest in the application of neuroscience to education. Furst (2018) has provided a useful synthesis of the key aspects of neuroscience that can be applied to education to help us understand how students learn. Neuroscience can play an important role in supporting us to understand how knowledge is stored in the memory and how new knowledge connects with prior knowledge to activate neural connections.

Furst (2018) presents a model which separates initial learning phases from subsequent 'practice' phases. The initial phases focus on explaining and supporting students to understand new concepts, perhaps using concrete examples. The practice phase establishes representations and builds retrieval pathways. During the process of retrieval, learners activate and reconstruct interconnected networks and pathways to locate relevant pieces of information. Furst (2018) divides the process of learning into the following phases.

- Knowing: the student learns a new concept. This results in new neural connections being formed between neurons in the brain.

- Understanding: the student connects the new concept to other concepts which have been established in the brain as neural connections.

- Using: the student can retrieve and use the new knowledge because pathways are built between neurons which facilitate retrieval.

- Applying: the new concept becomes part of a well-connected network of concepts which enables the learner to use the new information quickly and automatically.

IN THE CLASSROOM

To reduce overload on the working memory, teachers can use chunking. Subject-specific content can be broken down into small, manageable chunks. These might be referred to as 'components' of knowledge. Each lesson could focus on a single component. Teachers then teach each component of knowledge through explicit and direct instruction and provide guided opportunities for students to work on each component of knowledge before asking them to work on each component independently. The components of knowledge combine to form 'composite' knowledge. This is the endpoint of a unit of work. The composite knowledge is the knowledge that students need to know after all the components have been taught. Often, the composite knowledge is the starting point for planning. Teachers identify initially what they want students to know at the end of a unit of work. They then work backwards from this point to identify all the component knowledge that students need to reach the endpoint.

TAKE 5

- Environmental factors can influence the structure of the brain.

- The brain is malleable rather than static and good teaching can promote brain growth and intelligence.

- The working memory can hold multiple pieces of information, but it can only store it for a limited time.

- The long-term memory can hold information for a few minutes, months or even years, but that information must be retrieved.

- Retrieval tasks activate the long-term memory.

SUMMARY

This chapter has outlined the role of the working memory and long-term memory in students' learning. We have emphasised the importance of reducing cognitive load and the need to teach component knowledge explicitly and directly before asking students to work independently on subject content.

3
COGNITIVE LOAD

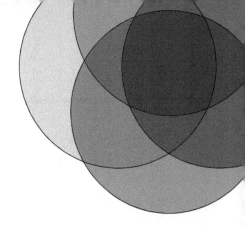

TEACHERS' STANDARDS

This chapter addresses TS2, which focuses on securing good student progress through understanding how children learn.

— IN THIS CHAPTER

This chapter revisits some of the information about memory that was outlined in Chapter 2 and goes into more detail about cognitive load. Practical strategies for reducing cognitive load are also outlined in this chapter. We emphasise the importance of breaking subject content down into small, manageable chunks and the importance of reducing extraneous content which increases cognitive load.

KEY POLICY DOCUMENTATION

The *ITT Core Content Framework* states that trainee teachers must learn that:

> *Working memory is where information that is being actively processed is held, but its capacity is limited and can be overloaded.*

(DfE, 2019a, p11)

COGNITIVE ARCHITECTURE

Humans take in information from their environment. This exposes them to an unlimited store of information. Information goes into our memory store. As discussed in Chapter 2, the memory is made up of our working memory and our long-term memory. The *working memory* is the part of the memory where all our thinking takes place (Lovell, 2020). It is limited in capacity. When we think about information and link it to prior knowledge, the information transfers from our working memory to our long-term memory. However, if we do not process or engage with the information in our working memory, the information is quickly forgotten.

In contrast, there is no capacity limit to the *long-term memory*. We store a range of information and experiences in our long-term memory including life events (episodic knowledge), factual information (semantic knowledge) and knowledge of how to complete tasks (procedural knowledge). It is an unlimited store of information (Lovell, 2020). Once information is stored in the long-term memory, it can be forgotten if it is not retrieved.

Cognitive load theory addresses techniques for managing working memory load in order to enable learners to process complex cognitive tasks (Paas et al., 2003). The aim is to reduce the load on the working memory so that it can function more efficiently. Teachers can reduce the load on the working memory by breaking down or 'chunking' information in manageable ways and by connecting new learning to previous learning. Research has also found that cognitive load in the classroom is exacerbated by adverse experiences that students are exposed to (Darling-Hammond et al., 2020). This is because the working memory is not only processing cognitive tasks, but also emotional responses to situations that may be adversely impacting on the child. An example of this is a student who is experiencing bullying. Their working memory may be processing what they will do after the lesson to keep themselves safe as well as trying to process the subject content in the lesson. This results in overload to the working memory. It is therefore essential that teachers consider cognitive load and the limitations of working memory. Teachers must ensure that learning experiences are designed and delivered in a way that reduces the load on working memory. This supports learners to process information and move it into long-term memory so that it can be stored for retrieval later. If teaching and learning activities overload a learner's working memory, then those activities will not directly contribute to learning.

CHUNKING AND AUTOMATING

Cognitive load is anything that takes up working memory capacity (Lovell, 2020). When we are taking in new information, this takes up more working memory capacity than when we are working with familiar information. Cognitively demanding tasks can overload the working memory. Think about when you learned how to drive. When learning to drive, there are many new things to remember. The steps are not automatic, and we need to consciously think about them. We must think about the processes involved in changing gears, for example – slowing down, pressing the clutch, moving down through the gears and so on. We must think consciously about using our mirrors and when to turn on the indicators. There are many steps that we need to remember. The driving instructor makes it easier for us by taking some control of some of the processes so that we can think about a limited number of skills rather than having to remember everything. This is called *chunking*. Chunking is when teachers break new information down into a series of small steps so that students can focus on a limited amount of new information rather than having to remember everything. When we have been driving for a while, the processes become automatic. We do not need to think about how we change gears; we just do it without thinking. We *automate* the new learning.

When learning becomes automatic, this reduces cognitive load and allows us to focus on other things. Let's think about a child who is learning to write. In the early stages of writing, young children need to remember a lot of new information. They must remember the words that they are writing in the sentence, how to spell words and how to form letters within words. In addition, they need to remember when to use punctuation and what type of punctuation to use. They also need to remember the order of the words in the sentence so that the sentence makes sense. They experience cognitive load because none of this knowledge has become automated. As they progress, much of this knowledge becomes automatic. They do not need to consciously think about letter formation, spelling or sentence structure. This frees up their working memory capacity so that their working memory can focus on the content of their writing (for example, developing an exciting plot in a story).

Now let's think of the processes involved in learning to read. Early readers experience a lot of cognitive load because they need to recognise graphemes, link graphemes to phonemes, blend phonemes together to read words (decoding) and when words cannot be read using their knowledge of phonics (exception words), they need to retrieve information from their semantic memory. Is there any wonder that they often cannot gain any meaning from the text they are reading? They are focusing on the smaller skills and all this effort is cognitively demanding and takes up working memory capacity. As they become skilled readers, the processes described above become automatic. They do not need to consciously think about them. This frees up working memory capacity so that they can think about the characters or the plot of the story.

iNTRiNSiC AND EXTRANEOUS COGNiTiVE LOAD

Lovell (2020) distinguishes between intrinsic and extraneous cognitive load. *Intrinsic cognitive load* is the load associated with new core learning – the concepts, knowledge and skills to be mastered. This core learning places a heavy burden on the working memory until it has been mastered and automated. Extraneous cognitive load is the type of load that teachers need to minimise. It results from the additional information that we present to students which is not essential to the core learning. Our priority as educators is for our students to focus on the core learning and not on other information which might be interesting but is not essential in supporting students' knowledge of subject-specific knowledge. According to Lovell (2020), this additional information diverts resources away from the working memory and therefore reduces the capacity of the working memory to process the core learning. *Total cognitive load* is the combination of intrinsic and extraneous load. Total cognitive load cannot exceed the capacity of the working memory. If it does, learning will not occur. Lovell (2020) refers to extraneous load as 'the froth of the learning task' (p260) – it is nice, but it is not essential and should only be included if it supports the core learning.

One approach which has gained popularity in recent years is based on dual coding theory. This is where teachers present information to students in a range of forms. An example is the use of diagrams and pictures to support written information. If the visual information supports the core learning, then this is not a problem. However, if the visual information detracts attention away from the core learning, this has the effect of increasing cognitive load and therefore has a negative impact on the core learning.

The more elements of new information that students are required to think about, the higher the cognitive load. If students are focusing on one new piece of information, this results in low cognitive load. However, if they are learning several pieces of new information at the same time, this results in high cognitive load. Let's consider a science investigation. The students have been tasked with designing an investigation to explore the effects of different electrical components on electrical current. There are a variety of skills that they need to think about. They need to generate a hypothesis, design the investigation so that it is fair, communicate their ideas with their peers, make predictions, collect and record results and confirm or disprove the hypothesis. Some of these skills are new, so they are cognitively demanding. However, their knowledge of the underpinning scientific concepts is not secure. This type of knowledge is substantive knowledge. This further increases the cognitive load. It would be more effective if the students had secure subject knowledge before attempting the investigation so that they can focus on developing the skills of working scientifically. This type of knowledge is known as disciplinary knowledge.

ELEMENT INTERACTIVITY

Element interactivity relates to the number of new elements of information that students are required to think about during a lesson or learning task. Increasing the number of new elements that we require students to think about results in higher cognitive load (Lovell, 2020). Element interactivity refers to the complexity of relations between these elements (Lovell, 2020). Material that has high element interactivity contains multiple elements that students are required to process simultaneously (Lovell, 2020).

CURRICULUM SEQUENCING

Well-designed sequences of learning can reduce cognitive load. Schools are now starting to classify knowledge into components and composites. *Component* knowledge is the tiny bite-sized chunks of knowledge that students need to learn within a subject. A well-designed curriculum introduces students to component knowledge in the right order so that students can connect new learning to existing learning. Several components combine to form composites. *Composite knowledge* is the knowledge that students learn after they have mastered the component knowledge. Composite knowledge can be made up of several components. Focusing our teaching so that we address the component knowledge first helps to reduce cognitive load. Teaching a lesson which requires students to understand several components can increase cognitive load. Teaching one component aspect of knowledge in a lesson can reduce cognitive load. Setting a task which requires students to understand components that they have not yet been taught will increase cognitive load.

SCHEDULING

Block scheduling is the practice of timetabling fewer but longer classes per day. This practice is thought to reduce cognitive load and anxiety for students (Darling-Hammond et al., 2020). Cognitive load refers to the amount of mental effort required in using working memory. If students are required to participate in four or five lessons each day, this places a significant load on the working memory. In this instance, students will need to draw on many different neural pathways in the brain as they switch from one lesson to the next. Reducing the number of lessons eases the cognitive load on the working memory and allows teachers to achieve greater depth in relation to subject-specific knowledge, understanding, application and synthesis.

THE PROBLEM WITH DISCOVERY LEARNING TASKS

Through using clear explanations and effective modelling in lessons, teachers can reduce the cognitive load on students. Cognitive load theory suggests that discovery learning, or unstructured learning, may generate a heavy working memory load that is detrimental to learning. This suggestion is particularly important in the case of students who lack proper schemas to integrate the new information with their prior knowledge (Kirschner et al., 2006).

PRE-TEACHING

Pre-teaching essential subject-specific concepts and knowledge can reduce cognitive load. Some students benefit greatly from this, particularly those with SEND or English as an Additional Language (EAL). If the lesson includes essential subject-specific concepts and knowledge (for example, new vocabulary, which is a common source of high cognitive load) that students need to learn, pre-teaching this before the lesson can reduce cognitive load. This is particularly important if several concepts or aspects of knowledge are being introduced in the lesson. According to Lovell (2020), 'If students experience high cognitive load when required to think about lots of *new* information at one time (high element interactivity), we can reduce the cognitive load of the overall task by pre-teaching' (p39).

KEY RESEARCH: SEGMENTATION

Breaking a task down into bite-sized chunks is known as the *isolated elements effect*. The approach is also known as segmentation. This reduces intrinsic cognitive load. This is where teachers provide first a task with a lower level of element interactivity followed by a more complete task with higher levels of element interactivity (Sweller et al., 2011).

KEY RESEARCH: THE REDUNDANCY EFFECT

According to Sweller et al. (2011), 'the most common form of redundancy occurs when the same information is presented in different modalities' (p142). Lovell (2020) provides an example of redundancy when presenters present the audience with written information and then read from their slides, thus supplying the audience with auditory information. Only one format is needed, either written or auditory information, not both, and therefore some information is not required – it is redundant. This is because the working memory processes all language in the same place, the phonological loop. Therefore, when information is presented simultaneously in written and spoken form, both forms are competing to be processed in the same part of the working memory. They are interfering with each other. Cognitive load is reduced when each component of the working memory only needs to process one 'piece' of information.

The second component of the working memory, the visuospatial sketch pad, processes visual and spatial information. It is used to support navigation skills and for processing visual information other than written words. Written words are processed in the phonological loop. It is possible for students to complete a task which uses both sub-sets of the working memory (i.e. the phonological loop and the visuospatial sketch pad) without overloading the working memory because the information is then processed in separate subsystems and is not competing to be processed in the same place. This explains why presenters who only include images on slides (rather than text) but then use the spoken word throughout their presentation can create high levels of engagement from the audience; the visual information is processed in one component of the working memory and the auditory information is processed in a separate component of the working memory. The different 'pieces' of information are not competing for the same space in the working memory.

Chandler and Sweller (1991) presented students with three diagrams of the heart. The first diagram showed the heart with each component labelled using very simple labels. The second diagram included a separate block of text which outlined the process of blood entering and leaving the heart. The third diagram overlaid this same text next to each component on the diagram. Different groups of students were allocated one of the diagrams and asked to study it. Following this, each group was required to complete a series of tasks which included labelling incomplete diagrams and answering questions about the heart. The students who were presented with the simple diagram performed better in all tasks than the other two groups.

iN THE CLASSROOM

Cognitive load can be reduced by:

- carefully sequencing subject content;
- breaking subject content into smaller chunks;
- teaching subject content through direct explicit instruction;
- guiding students initially as they begin to work on subject content;
- not introducing independent work until students are secure with subject content;
- fading out scaffolding to gradually increase student independence;
- revisiting subject content;
- using retrieval practice;
- ensuring that students understand subject-specific content before they do an enquiry task.

TAKE 5

- The working memory has limited capacity. This means that teachers should limit the amount of information they introduce in lessons so that cognitive load is reduced.
- Information transfers from the working memory to the long-term memory.
- Information that is stored in the long-term memory needs to be retrieved so that it becomes automated.
- Scaffolding and fading can be used to gradually increase student independence.
- Pre-teaching subject content can reduce cognitive load.

SUMMARY

This chapter has provided theoretical and practical information about cognitive load. Reducing cognitive load is really just common sense. Human beings can only process a limited amount of information at any one time. Chunking content into component knowledge and then carefully sequencing those components will maximise learning because this ensures that students are not being asked to think about lots of different things at once. One of the challenges of achieving this is restricted curriculum time in school and the pressure on teachers to cover large syllabus content. One way of addressing this is for schools to use blended approaches to learning by making good use of virtual learning platforms for asynchronous content, although this approach requires further research.

4

CLASSROOM PRACTICE

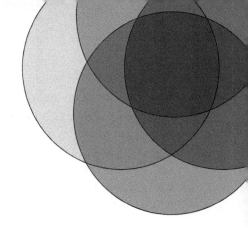

TEACHERS' STANDARDS

This chapter addresses elements of TS4, which focuses on planning and teaching well-structured lessons.

IN THIS CHAPTER

Schools and the education sector more generally have recently started to focus on the extent to which cognitive science can inform classroom practice. This chapter focuses mainly on the application of cognitive science in the classroom, although other aspects are discussed. It applies cognitive science specifically to five aspects of classroom practice: spaced learning, interleaving, retrieval practice, cognitive load and dual coding. Other classroom strategies are considered, including the role of direct teaching, modelling, questioning and metacognition in promoting learning.

It is important to emphasise that different educational contexts, including schools, classrooms, age phases and even subjects, will influence the extent to which specific strategies can be successfully applied. Schools are complex organisations and learning can be influenced by a myriad of factors. In addition, research on the application of cognitive science in the classroom is at an early stage. Currently, studies are limited to specific subjects, age phases and learning outcomes (EEF, 2021) and there is a paucity of evidence to support the application of cognitive science across all subjects and age ranges. It is also important to emphasise that some strategies have not been effectively applied in classrooms, resulting in negative impacts on learning (EEF, 2021). It is therefore important to proceed with caution. That said, insights from cognitive psychology and cognitive neuroscience, particularly in relation to the sciences of the mind and the brain, can usefully inform classroom practice and some of the studies which apply cognitive science to classroom contexts do show promising results.

Cognitive science can usefully inform a variety of educational approaches. However, insights from more traditional learning theories should not be debunked, particularly socio-constructivist approaches to learning and embodied learning. Indeed, we think that strategies informed by cognitive science and more traditional sociocultural perspectives on learning and development are not mutually exclusive and that they might be complementary. The effectiveness of any classroom strategy is likely to be influenced by the age of the students, the subject, students' prior knowledge and the teacher. There is no guarantee that any strategy will be successful, but the strategies outlined in this chapter each warrant due consideration.

KEY POLICY DOCUMENTATION

This chapter draws heavily on the following report:

Education Endowment Foundation (2021) *Cognitive Science Approaches in the Classroom: A Review of the Evidence*, London: EEF.

DIRECT TEACHING AND MODELLING

Two different types of modelling are described in the literature.

- Mastery models demonstrate rapid learning and make no errors. In this type of modelling, the teacher models the task or skill perfectly.

- Coping models are not perfect. Teachers show their hesitations and make errors so that they demonstrate approaching the task from the perspective of the pupil.

(Braaksma et al., 2002)

Research has demonstrated that the use of mastery (competent) models is more effective than coping models (Graham and Harris, 1994; Schunk et al., 1987). However, the research is inconclusive. Evidence in other studies suggests that weak learners learn more from focusing their observations on weak models, but better learners learn more from focusing on good models (Braaksma et al., 2002). Braaksma et al. (2002) suggest this is likely to be the case because accurate models are more matched with the cognitive processes of a good learner and a weak model is probably more matched with the cognitive processes of a weak learner.

Regardless of these research findings, it could be argued that students of all abilities should be introduced to accurate models so that they can aspire to replicate them. However, there is also value in students observing coping models. Coping models provide an opportunity for teachers to model misconceptions and to model the process of thinking like a learner.

IN THE CLASSROOM

Teachers can model subject content on the whiteboard, using the visualiser or through demonstrating a skill using subject-specific resources. The key to success is to ensure that the subject content is not just explained to the students but that it is also demonstrated very explicitly.

SCAFFOLDING

During the process of scaffolding, teachers support students to master subject content before students are required to work on subject content independently. This support enables students to become confident with the subject content. The support is gradually faded out and students are then required to work independently on the subject content. This is known as fading.

IN THE CLASSROOM

Teachers can scaffold learning through:

- providing worked examples;
- guiding the students through the steps in a problem after they have modelled the steps first;
- providing students with graphic organisers to support them to structure their work;
- asking students to work in pairs on a problem before they work independently on similar problems.

QUESTIONING

Questioning is an essential teaching skill both to check understanding and to promote thinking. The most effective questions promote higher-level thinking rather than closed responses. Examples of good questions might include the following:

- How do you know that?
- Can you justify your answer?
- Can you explain this to me?

IN THE CLASSROOM

Hinge questions are effective in determining the direction of a lesson. They enable teachers to know if subject content that has just been taught in a lesson has been understood or not, and therefore they help teachers to decide whether to go in one direction or another, that is whether to re-teach the subject content or whether to move on to the next step. The process is outlined below.

- The teacher models the subject content through explicit direct instruction.

- The teacher asks a hinge question. This should promote a whole class response, either through a choral response, or through asking students to write down a response to the question before showing the teacher their response.

- If the students have given the correct response, the teacher moves on to the next step.

- If many students have misunderstood and produced an incorrect response, the teacher re-teaches the content.

- Hinge questions should be quick checks of the learning – they should be completed within a very short amount of time.

SPACED LEARNING

Spaced practice is sometimes referred to as distributed practice or distributed learning. It applies the principle that material is more easily learnt when it is spaced out over time with deliberate intervals of time inserted between taught content (EEF, 2021). In effect, this means that substantive content is introduced and then revisited and developed further at a subsequent point in a learning sequence following an interval. During the interval, the students move on to learn different content. This allows them to almost forget content which has been previously introduced. However, they will revisit that content after the interval and build on it so that learning is not lost. An example is shown in Figure 4.1, using chemistry as an example.

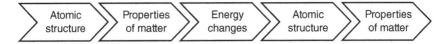

Figure 4.1   Example of distributed learning over a sequence of lessons or units

This approach contrasts with blocked practice or clustered practice where material is introduced sequentially. An example of this approach is shown in Figure 4.2.

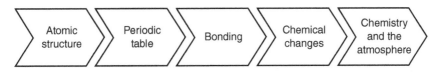

Figure 4.2   Example of clustered practice over a sequence of lessons or units

Spaced learning is more challenging for students, as it prevents information being held in the working memory (EEF, 2021). However, revisiting substantive and disciplinary knowledge over longer periods of time increases long-term retention and increases the likelihood of information being held in the long-term memory (EEF, 2021). During the intervals, students are taught unrelated content. Evidence suggests that spacing content across days or lessons rather than spacing content within individual lessons produces a small positive impact (EEF, 2021). Students might revisit a subject-specific concept several times over one week or several weeks or content could be spaced out across a term or even a school year. This practice forces students to retrieve information from their long-term memory, and therefore spacing is often combined with retrieval practice.

One of the challenges of distributed practice is that curricula in schools is often organised into blocks. This is often referred to as 'clustered' practice, whereby subject content is taught sequentially with no opportunities to revisit that content. Schools may therefore need to think differently about curriculum design by moving away from rigidly planned blocked learning.

Spaced learning or distributed practice within lessons is less common. This is where subject content is introduced and repeated several times within a lesson but broken up by intervals where the teacher addresses unrelated content. There is limited research on the effectiveness of this strategy, but small-scale studies suggest that this strategy may have a positive impact on learning (EEF, 2021). Figure 4.3 illustrates how this approach might look within a single science lesson.

KEY RESEARCH

Evidence suggests that although distributed practice makes learning more difficult (EEF, 2021), it is likely to lead to long-term retention of subject content. This is because it challenges students to revisit information that has been almost forgotten, thus activating the long-term memory. Long-term retention of knowledge is supported if learning is spread out, with gaps in between to allow forgetting. This 'is one of the most general and robust effects from across the entire history of experimental research on learning and memory' (Bjork and Bjork, 2011, p59).

IN THE CLASSROOM

Sam introduces students to the concept of 'class' in a history lesson. He elicits the students' understanding of class, but at this stage, their understanding is basic in that they associate class with wealth. Sam deliberately revisits the concept of class over several lessons. In some lessons, he decides not to address the concept, instead focusing on different concepts. In the lessons where he deliberately chooses to address class, he activates students' prior

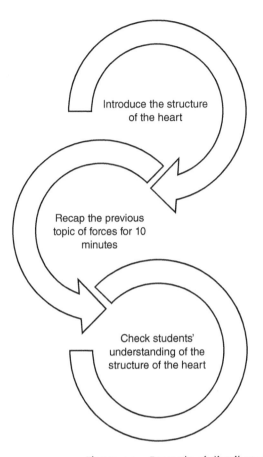

Figure 4.3   Example of distributed learning within lessons

understanding of this concept and then develops their understanding further. After several lessons, the students have a more developed understanding of class.

iNTERLEAViNG

Interleaving subject content with other tasks or topics leads to better long-term retention and transfer of skills (Bjork and Bjork, 2011). Evidence suggests that this strategy is particularly effective with learners aged 8–14 (EEF, 2021). Interleaving is the practice of interspersing learning material, such as tasks or subject content, with slightly different content or activities. It is sometimes referred to as 'mixed' or 'varied' practice. The tasks or content that are interspersed are not completely different to those which have been introduced. This approach differs to spaced or distributed practice which uses intervals that are filled with unrelated activities (EEF, 2021).

Interleaving challenges students to think hard because the content or tasks which are introduced in the lesson are related but different. Students are therefore required to make comparisons between different types of tasks and develop more complex schemas. It is a strategy that is well suited to problem-solving tasks (EEF, 2021) which require students to select strategies to generate solutions. Switching between different types of tasks requires students to differentiate between the different tasks and when interleaved items are very similar but different, this increases the level of challenge. However, the approach should be used with caution. It is possible that interleaving could result in some students becoming confused or disengaged in lessons. It is also important that students are secure with subject-specific content before using interleaving. Figure 4.4 provides an example of interleaving.

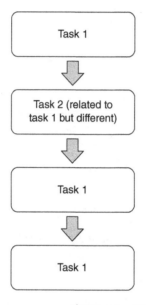

Figure 4.4   Example of interleaving within lessons

The benefits of interleaving appear to depend on the mixing of related but different items (Kornell and Bjork, 2008). One study (Hausman and Kornell, 2014) interleaved unrelated items and found no benefit. However, research suggests that interleaving is especially effective when differences between items are subtle (Carvalho and Goldstone, 2014). There is inevitable spacing between tasks or content when interleaving, but interleaving is not the same as spaced practice where content that is introduced sequentially is unrelated. The spacing effect boosts memory, but although it may lead to better outcomes in the long term, it may hinder performance in the short term. The key is that the interleaved items cannot be too different but nor can they be too similar. Introducing two related but different tasks improves learning gains, even though students may spend less time on each task than when tasks are introduced through blocked instruction. Interleaving can be used within lessons or across a sequence of lessons.

iN THE CLASSROOM

In a chemistry lesson, students are provided with simple equations to balance. These are shown below.

$$2Cu + O_2 \rightarrow$$

$$2Cu + \quad \rightarrow 2CuO$$

$$+ O_2 \rightarrow 2CuO$$

The tasks require student to balance each of the equations, so the content is related. However, students are required to think differently as they work on each equation. This is an example of interleaving.

RETRiEVAL PRACTiCE

Retrieval practice is the process of recalling information from the long-term memory. Evidence from cognitive science suggests that when content is studied and recalled from the memory, memory strength increases (EEF, 2021). In addition, evidence suggests that *testing* learning supports learning and is often more effective than re-learning content that has previously been taught (EEF, 2021). Retrieval tasks make students aware of weaknesses in their memory and gaps in their understanding, thus supporting metacognitive skills. If students are aware that there are gaps in their learning, they can start to set goals and use self-monitoring strategies to support them in addressing learning gaps. Low-stakes quizzes and tasks are often used in lessons to support retrieval of information that has previously been taught. Examples include:

- multiple-choice questions;
- short answer questions;
- true/false questions;
- labelling diagrams;
- matching definitions to terms;
- writing a list;
- talking to a partner about a specific aspect of prior learning;
- quick sorting activities which require students to sort information into categories;
- cloze procedure tasks;
- class voting activities using technology.

Evidence generally demonstrates that retrieval practices have a positive impact on students' learning compared to the use of no retrieval (EEF, 2021). When retrieval activities identify both gaps in knowledge and subject-specific misconceptions, this provides an opportunity for the teacher to address these directly with students. The strategy can be combined with spaced practice.

iN THE CLASSROOM

Students in relationships education have been learning about the key signs of an unhealthy relationship, with a focus on manipulation and control. In the first lesson, they are introduced to the characteristics of unhealthy relationships. In the second lesson, the teacher wants to check that students have remembered the key signs of an unhealthy relationship. At the start of the lesson, the teacher asks the students to work in groups. She has provided each group with a large sheet of flip-chart paper and pens. She asks the students to list the key signs of unhealthy relationships and she gives them three minutes to complete this task. The teacher then checks each group's response to the task.

COGNiTiVE LOAD

The working memory is limited in capacity. The amount of information held in the working memory varies between individuals, but typically it can hold approximately four or five pieces of information. When learners are presented with a large amount of complex information, particularly if information is new and has not been committed to the long-term memory, the working memory might become overwhelmed, resulting in cognitive load.

The evidence on cognitive load is promising and there are many studies which demonstrate that the use of worked examples can reduce cognitive load (EEF, 2021). However, there is limited research on the use of worked examples in subjects other than mathematics and English.

It is important that teachers understand cognitive load and particularly strategies to reduce overloading students' working memories. Examples of strategies include:

- breaking down content into a series of manageable chunks;

- providing students with complete or partially complete worked examples;

- providing students with step-by-step instructions;

- using diagrams to illustrate the steps through a problem;

- providing students with templates, guidance and helpful prompts or cues to reduce the information that they need to remember;

- working in pairs or small groups during lessons: collaborative working, however, can increase cognitive load if students do not work together effectively and are unclear about their roles within a collaborative task (EEF, 2021);

- fading: gradually reducing the level of information provided by worked examples;

- using incorrect worked examples and asking students to identify the errors: evidence suggests that this strategy has a positive effect on higher attaining students, but research findings are less conclusive for lower attaining students (EEF, 2021).

iN THE CLASSROOM

In physics, the students are required to calculate speed, distance and time. The students are provided with word problems. To reduce cognitive load, the teacher provides the students with the equations for speed, distance and time so that students do not have to think about the process for each type of problem. They are simply required to apply the equation.

Scaffolding can take a variety of forms, but the overall purpose of scaffolding is to provide students with support while they engage with a task. This support can gradually be reduced (fading) as students develop increased competence with the task. Examples of scaffolding include the use of prompts, cues, instructions, definitions of key vocabulary and templates to reduce the burden on the working memory, thus reducing cognitive load as a student completes a task. However, teachers should be aware that students can become reliant on scaffolds and that students with strong foundational knowledge are less likely to benefit from them (EEF, 2021).

USiNG CONCRETE REPRESENTATiONS

Practical resources, including models and manipulatives, can support students to understand abstract subject content. For example, it is difficult for students to understand the structure of an atom or a molecule in chemistry because we cannot see these things in everyday life. A concrete representation such as a model of an atom or molecule can aid students' understanding. Models and other representations are widely used in science, but they can also be used in other subjects. The use of globes in geography can aid children's understanding of scale. Consider how models, images and manipulatives might be used across the secondary curriculum to support students' understanding.

iN THE CLASSROOM

- In chemistry, students are learning about the properties of solids, liquids and gasses. In each lesson, the teacher refers to a physical model which helps students understand the structure of solids, liquids and gasses.

- In biology, students are provided with a physical model of the heart so that they can identify the location of the chambers, the arteries and the veins.

- In mathematics, the teacher demonstrates fraction equivalence using a model which represents a fraction wall, and using models of 'pizzas' to illustrate the relationship between different fractions.

SCHEMAS

Schemas are structures that organise knowledge in the mind. One way of understanding this is to think of the mind as a filing cabinet with separate folders. The folders are a way of organising the information into logical categories. The information in each category or folder is connected in some way. When we learn something, new knowledge is connected to pre-existing knowledge, and this results in initial schemas being modified. Schemas are not fixed, but there are pedagogical approaches that teachers can use to support students to make connections between pre-existing knowledge and developing knowledge. These include:

- concept/knowledge mapping and organisation;

- schema/concept comparison and cognitive conflict.

Concept maps and knowledge organisers may help students to organise knowledge and extend schemas (EEF, 2021), particularly if students keep updating them during a unit of work. These documents can be revisited regularly by students and used for self-testing. They frequently take the format of a mind map to summarise and organise key ideas. Concept maps are visual representations created by students or teachers to connect ideas, concepts and terms. Students can use them to organise information they already know and to incorporate new learning with this prior knowledge. They can typically include pictures, drawings and diagrams. A knowledge organiser captures all the essential information about topics studied in any given subject. The knowledge organiser allows students to see immediately the fundamental knowledge they need to succeed in lessons and examinations.

Schema conflict, or cognitive conflict, is a psychological state involving a discrepancy between pre-existing schemas and new knowledge. Classroom tasks that require students to compare contrasting, complementary or conflicting concepts or examples have generated mixed findings in research studies (EEF, 2021). However, this strategy can address subject-specific misconceptions and result in modification of pre-existing schemas.

iN THE CLASSROOM

The students are learning about the Second World War in history. The students are provided with a knowledge organiser. This outlines the following aspects:

- Chronology: the events on a timeline leading to the outbreak of the war, including significant events during the war that students need to remember.

- Key facts: the important facts that students need to remember.

- Important people: the significant individuals that students need to know.

- Key quotes: an example could include a famous quote from Winston Churchill.

- Key vocabulary: the key words that students need to know and remember, for example, the Blitz.

MULTIMEDIA LEARNING AND DUAL CODING

The working memory processes visual and spatial information via the visuospatial sketch pad and auditory information via the phonological loop. Dual coding theory is based on the assumption that if information is presented to students in multiple formats, these formats utilise both subsystems of the working memory, thus meaning that the working memory is being fully utilised and is working to full capacity. It is important to understand that:

- there are two separate channels for information in the working memory and this is known as dual coding theory. These channels are the visuospatial sketch pad and the phonological loop. Each of these components of the working memory deals with different types of information;

- each component of the working memory has a finite capacity;

- learning is an active process of working with this information.

(EEF, 2021)

Teachers may deliberately decide to support auditory information with illustrations, diagrams, visualisations or simulation activities.

Visual representation and illustration: Many of the studies on visual representations and illustrations (additional images, pictures or icons that symbolise, illustrate or represent content) have reported positive effects, although some studies have reported no effect or harmful effects (EEF, 2021). It is important that images are designed to provide students with information rather than serving decorative purposes to reduce cognitive load. When irrelevant illustrations are added to presentations, this may be a distraction and increase cognitive load rather than supporting the development of schemas (EEF, 2021).

Diagrams: Diagrams represent relevant concepts or phenomena and are different to visual representations and illustrations. They help students to understand subject-specific concepts and they provide useful summaries of learning. Again, most research studies have demonstrated positive effects, but some show null or negative effects (EEF, 2021).

Spatial, visualisation and simulation approaches: These approaches support students to imagine learning content. Research evidence demonstrates small to moderate positive effects (EEF, 2021) and therefore this strategy shows promise.

IN THE CLASSROOM

In a history lesson, students are asked to close their eyes or wear blindfolds. The teacher then plays the sound of an air raid siren. The students listen to it. The teacher then introduces them to the sound of bombs and aeroplanes. This is a simulation activity. Following the activity, students are asked to describe how it might have felt to experience a blackout during the Second World War.

How might simulation be used in other subjects?

How might technology be used to facilitate access to simulation activities?

EMBODIED LEARNING

Embodied learning is the use of movement and the body to support students' understanding of subject-specific concepts and ideas. This pedagogical approach assumes that there is a connection between the mind and the body. It includes the use of movement, gestures and actions. Evidence from research studies shows that this strategy has a consistently positive effect on learning (EEF, 2021), although almost all the studies have been conducted in primary schools. There is limited evidence on its application in secondary schools. It is important that the pedagogical approaches support students' understanding rather than distracting them and increasing cognitive load.

METACOGNITIVE STRATEGIES

Metacognition is the process of learning how to learn. It involves the skills of identifying goals, planning how to achieve these, self-monitoring and evaluating learning so that students achieve the best outcomes. Effective learners use these metacognitive strategies all the time and they are lifelong skills.

Teachers can enable metacognitive strategies by modelling how to:

- check the accuracy of tasks that have been attempted;
- use checklists (success criteria) to monitor the quality of work during completion of a task;
- edit work to improve it;

- self-evaluate work against the success criteria;

- plan how to approach a specific task.

This is not an exhaustive list. The key point is that effective learners are strategic learners. They can use the skills of goal setting, planning, monitoring and evaluating to meet deadlines and achieve goals and to improve the quality of their work. Teachers need to explicitly model these strategies because they are not always intuitive.

iN THE CLASSROOM

Students are asked to complete a project in geography. The project builds on subject content that has been taught and enables students to develop their skills in geographical enquiry. The students are asked to work in pairs to plan a geographical enquiry. They are required to identify goals, plan their work, carry out their investigation, monitor their own progress and evaluate their learning. They are required to produce a geographical report that outlines the process of their enquiry.

TAKE 5

- Hinge questions enable teachers to make decisions about whether to re-teach subject content within a lesson or to move on to something new.

- Spacing out learning over time with gaps in between to allow learners to forget what they have been taught then revisiting that content leads to gains in learning.

- Retrieval activities enable students to remember subject content.

- Direct and explicit instruction reduces cognitive load rather than enquiry-based approaches that increase cognitive load, particularly if students are not secure with subject content before they undertake an enquiry task.

- Interleaving subject content with related but different content makes learning more difficult in the short term but leads to better long-term retention.

SUMMARY

Although the evidence for the application of cognitive science in classrooms has produced mixed results, some studies have yielded positive results, which demonstrates that specific pedagogical approaches show promise. The research on interleaving has almost exclusively been conducted in mathematics and there is a lack of research about its application across a range of subjects and age phases. Research on dual coding is also inconclusive and demonstrates how it is possible to implement the strategy poorly, resulting in increases rather than reductions to cognitive load. Despite the lack of research on applied cognitive science, we are not asserting that these approaches are not effective. We are emphasising the need for more research to be conducted. There is value in teachers knowing about the principles of cognitive science, including spaced learning, worked examples, scaffolding and verbal and visual representation of information, because there is evidence, albeit in specific contexts, to demonstrate that these can positively influence rates of learning and retention of information.

5
RETRiEVAL PRACTiCE

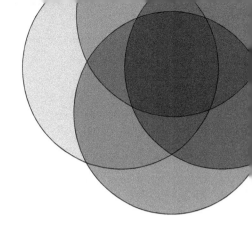

TEACHERS' STANDARDS

This chapter addresses TS2 and TS4. These standards focus on how children learn and on classroom practice.

---
iN THiS CHAPTER

Most of us have studied for high-stakes examinations at school. We were taught the subject content for the examinations, we revised that subject content and then we took the examination. However, regardless of the examination results we achieved, many of us struggle to recall the subject content that we were taught several years after taking the examinations. The information goes into long-term memory. However, if we do not retrieve that information regularly and process it, then it does not become automated. To make knowledge 'stick', it is essential that we retrieve it regularly and do something with it. This chapter outlines the importance of retrieval practice in schools. It outlines what retrieval practice is and it provides some practical strategies for teachers to use in the classroom. We emphasise that low-stakes quizzes are particularly effective in supporting retrieval of subject content. However, these are not the only approach. There are numerous strategies that teachers can use to facilitate retrieval.

KEY POLICY DOCUMENTATiON

The *ITT Core Content Framework* states that trainees must learn that:

> *Regular purposeful practice of what has previously been taught can help consolidate material and help pupils remember what they have learned.*

(DfE, 2019a, p12)

DOES LEARNiNG 'SiNK iN'?

Kate Jones (2019) reminds us that learning does not just sink in. For learning to stick, it requires some conscious effort, some practice and some determination. The working memory is limited in capacity. It enables us to complete tasks and it is the place where we process new information. However, if we do not do anything with that information, then we will quickly lose it. Jones (2019) argues that we must practise remembering to learn new information.

Not only do we lose information from our working memory, but we also lose information from our long-term memory. For information to become integrated into the long-term memory, it must be assimilated into existing schemas or used to modify existing schemas in some way. However, if that information is not retrieved, it does not become cemented in the long-term memory.

WHAT iS RETRiEVAL PRACTiCE?

Retrieval practice is the practice of recalling information from the long-term memory as a tool to promote learning, not as an assessment tool. Roediger and Karpicke (2006) are both influential academics working in the field of retrieval practice. They emphasise the powerful role of testing to improve learning. This has become known as the 'testing effect'. Essentially, this means that testing can support students to know and understand information that has been stored better. It can also help students to identify gaps in their knowledge, thus promoting further study. The use of tests to support retrieval is only one form of retrieval practice. Retrieval can be facilitated using questioning in a wide range of other activities that do not involve testing. However, it is important to emphasise that where tests are used to support retrieval, they are low-stakes tests. The purpose is not to elicit grades, but simply to identify what students know and don't know. The information gained from these tests can be used to inform subsequent teaching and also be used by students to guide their further study.

MEMORY

New information is stored for a very short time in our working memory. The capacity of the working memory is low and the length of time that information can be stored there varies from a few seconds to a few minutes (Jones, 2019), unless we process that information in some way. If information in the working memory is rehearsed, it can then be stored in the long-term memory. Jones (2019) differentiates between *retrieval storage*, which refers to how well information is embedded in the long-term memory, and *retrieval strength*, which relates to how well information can be retrieved when required. When information becomes automated in the long-term memory, it becomes part of our *procedural memory*. Information becomes automated when we do not need to consciously think about the information. An example of this is when a process becomes so automatic that we do not need to think about the steps involved in completing the task. The information that we hold about how to fasten our shoelaces becomes automatic and enters the procedural memory. However, when we are learning how to fasten our shoelaces, our knowledge of the processes is not automatic, and we must keep practising the skill by retrieving the information from our long-term memory. Procedural memory is important because when a process becomes automatic, it frees up the memory storage space so that we can focus on learning new information. New information is then transferred to the long-term memory (providing that we have rehearsed it or practised it immediately) and then we need to continue retrieving it from the long-term memory until that information can be stored in the procedural memory.

Kirschner et al. (2006) defined learning as a change in the long-term memory. They stated:

> If nothing has changed in long-term memory, nothing has been learned. Any instructional recommendation that does not or cannot specify what has been changed in long-term memory, or that does not increase the efficiency with which relevant information is stored in or retrieved from long-term memory, is likely to be ineffective.

> (Kirschner et al., 2006, p77)

Learning should result in modification to the cognitive structures within the memory. Schemas are mental representations that are formed within the memory. They are a convenient way of making sense of information and organising and categorising it. New learning results in schema modification. This is when new information is connected to information that has been previously stored in the long-term memory. New information often does not 'fit' automatically with previously stored information, so the schema must be modified to accommodate the new information. The information is stored within the schema but must be retrieved so that it does not get lost. Think of a ring binder folder full of our notes. The folder is the schema. It is a way of conveniently organising the information and we may use dividers to organise the information logically within the folder. When we learn new information, we write it down and insert it into the folder. That is where it is stored. However, if we never open that folder again to pull out the information, then we quite simply forget the information that we have stored in the folder. To remember the information, it is necessary to go back into the folder regularly, to re-read our notes and even to use self-testing techniques. This is exactly how our memory works, and this example illustrates nicely why retrieval is so important. Eventually, when we know the information well, it is stored in our procedural memory permanently and it becomes so automatic that we do not need to think about it. This frees up our working memory so that we can learn new information.

Jones (2019) argues that retrieval practice should be part of any knowledge-rich curriculum. According to Horvath (2019), 'every time you retrieve a memory it becomes deeper, stronger and easier to access in the future'. Testing not only identifies gaps in knowledge, it forces students to study the material as they prepare to take the test. However, after taking the test, if they re-study the material, they learn more than if they had simply re-studied the material without taking the test (Roediger and Karpicke, 2006).

BACKWARD TESTING EFFECT

A prominent direct benefit of testing is the (backward) testing effect, which refers to the finding that when participants repeatedly retrieve as opposed to re-study previously studied material, the retrieved items are better recalled on a delayed test than the re-studied items (Hogan and Kintsch, 1971; Roediger and Karpicke, 2006). The backward testing effect has been demonstrated across a wide range of settings (Karpicke, 2017).

FORWARD TESTING EFFECT

The forward testing effect is a more recent discovery (Pastötter and Bäuml, 2019). Testing previously learned material has also been shown to promote better learning of subsequent new material. This is known as the forward testing effect. An example is when students are tested for vocabulary that they have previously studied. This then leads to better learning of *new* vocabulary presented after the test. This is known as the forward testing effect.

KEY RESEARCH

Peterson and Peterson (1959) conducted research on the working memory that is now seminal. They found that information that is stored in the working memory, which is not rehearsed, is lost within 18–30 seconds. Consider the implications of this research for you as a teacher.

FORGETTING

Jones (2019) reminds us that forgetting is a key part of the learning process and that teachers should plan for this to happen. It is frustrating when students forget information that we have spent many hours preparing for them to learn. However, if stored information is not activated, retrieved and re-studied, then it will become forgotten forever. One seminal piece of work is Ebbinghaus's forgetting curve, which was published in 1885! The curve demonstrates that when information is taught, 100 per cent of that information is immediately remembered. After 20 minutes, this reduces to a little over 50 per cent, and after six days, the retention is just over 25 per cent. When we check to see if students have retained the information at the end of a lesson, the amount of information retained should be quite high. However, if we leave it too long to check retention, then much of the information will already be forgotten and will need to be re-studied.

KEY RESEARCH

Research by John Dunlosky et al. (2013) demonstrated that the following strategies are effective:

- practice testing or self-testing;

- distributed practice;

- interleaving;

- elaboration;

- self-explanation.

Less effective strategies were:

- re-reading material: this strategy does increase students' familiarity with the information, but it does not tell us whether information has been learned;

- highlighting key words and phrases: this activity is enjoyable for students but lacks challenge and doesn't deepen the memory;

- writing summaries of learning: younger students struggle with writing effective summaries and therefore this strategy might be more effective with older students.

(Dunlosky et al., 2013)

WHEN TO USE RETRIEVAL

Retrieval practice can be implemented in single lessons, across a sequence of lessons or unit of work and even across a year. Within a lesson, Rosenshine's (2010, 2012) first principle of instruction is to start a lesson with a review of previous learning. This could be a retrieval activity such as a low-stakes multiple-choice quiz, a task where students are required to match terms to definitions or sort information into categories, or it could be a quick task in which students are asked to write down everything they remember from the last lesson. They could spend a few minutes talking to their partner about the information they can remember from the previous lesson, or they could be given a mind map or concept map to complete. The key point to emphasise is that retrieval activities should be short, sharp and snappy. They should not take too much time and they are most effective when the teacher gains rapid information about each student's retention. Rosenshine (2010, 2012) emphasises the need to continually check students' understanding. This checking can be done during individual lessons, across a sequence of lessons, across a unit of work or across a year, and retrieval tasks can support this process. Rosenshine (2010, 2012) also emphasises the need for students to regularly review their learning. This process of reviewing learning can be supported by retrieval tasks that provide students with information about the knowledge they have retained and where there are gaps in their knowledge.

Tom Sherrington (2019a) argues that:

- students need to know in advance the knowledge that they will be expected to retrieve. Teachers can do this by informing students which items of knowledge a test will focus on;

- students need to know what items are held in their memory. Teachers should therefore not allow students to access prompts, cue cards and 'cheat sheets' (Jones, 2019) during a retrieval activity;

- retrieval activities should be varied so that students do not become disengaged;

- retrieval tasks should be designed so that they are time and workload efficient;

- students need to know what they got right and what they got wrong from a retrieval activity.

KEy RESEARCH

Research demonstrates that retrieval practice benefits low- and high-attaining students, including students with SEND (Roediger et al., 2011). In addition, dual coding theory has also shown promise. Research demonstrates that students can recall more information when they receive explanations using both words and images (De Bruyckere, 2018), providing that the images support students' understanding of the text and do not serve decorative purposes. It they are simply included to improve presentation, this can increase cognitive load. It is also important to note that dual coding theory is not a branch of learning styles theory. Learning styles theory has been debunked and therefore dual coding must not be confused with it.

iN THE CLASSRooM

Teachers can provide students with a series of low-stakes weekly quizzes that students complete during a unit of work. Multiple-choice quizzes are particularly effective, and many are automatically scored, thus ensuring that teachers do not have additional workload. Quizzes can be made available for students to complete in their own time or they can be used within lessons. They can be set so that students automatically receive a score when they submit their responses and students can be encouraged to re-take the quiz to increase their score. Teachers can have access to the results of each student and the whole class. This can provide information to the teacher which can inform decisions about whether subject content needs to be revisited in lessons.

TAKE 5

- If information is not retrieved and processed from the long-term memory, then students are likely to forget it.
- Multiple-choice quizzes are particularly effective in facilitating retrieval.
- Retrieval tasks can be used at the start of lessons or throughout lessons.
- Talk partner activities, sorting and matching activities, completing mind maps or 'list it' activities also facilitate retrieval.
- Use a range of retrieval activities to prevent disengagement.

SUMMARY

This chapter has outlined the importance of retrieval activities. It has presented some of the key research on retrieval and it has provided a range of pedagogical approaches for facilitating retrieval in the classroom.

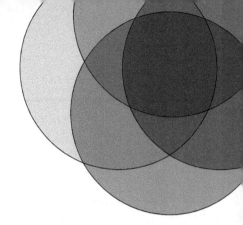

6
EXPLiCiT AND DiRECT iNSTRUCTiON

TEACHERS' STANDARDS

This chapter addresses elements of TS4, which focuses on planning and teaching well-structured lessons.

━━ iN THiS CHAPTER ━━━━━━━━━━━━━━━━━━━━━━━━━━━━━━━━━━━━━━

This chapter outlines the importance of explicit direct instruction in secondary schools. If we want students to learn something, then we need to teach them directly. Specific components of direct instruction are identified in this chapter, including chunking, modelling scaffolding, fading and independent practice. We outline the relationship between Rosenshine's principles and direct instruction (Rosenshine, 2010, 2012) and highlight the links between research and classroom practice.

KEY POLICY DOCUMENTATION

The *ITT Core Content Framework* states that trainees must learn that:

> *Effective teachers introduce new material in steps, explicitly linking new ideas to what has been previously studied and learned.*

(DfE, 2019a, p7)

This framework also emphasises the importance of modelling, scaffolding, questioning and repeated practice. All these strategies form essential components of explicit and direct instruction.

KEY RESEARCH

Research demonstrates that enthusiasm for 'discovery learning', where students discover knowledge for themselves, is not supported by research evidence, which broadly favours direct instruction (Kirschner et al., 2006). According to Coe et al. (2014), 'although learners do need to build new understanding on what they already know, if teachers want them to learn new ideas, knowledge or methods they need to teach them directly' (p23).

WHAT DO WE MEAN BY DIRECT INSTRUCTION?

The education sector uses a variety of associated terms for direct teaching, including explicit teaching, explicit instruction, direct instruction and teacher-led instruction. Direct teaching should not be confused with *didactic teaching*, which often results in students being passive learners. It requires a high level of student engagement in the process of learning to maximise the success rate.

Direct instruction involves chunking content into small components, guiding students' initial attempts at working with subject content and gradually releasing control to enable students to develop mastery of the subject content (Ashman, 2019a). It is often characterised by the following structure:

- I do: the teacher models and explains the subject content.

- We do: the teacher and students practise the content together.

- You do: the students work independently on the content.

(Adapted from Ashman, 2019a, p31)

According to Ashman (2019a), the principles of direct teaching contradict those of enquiry-based learning models. In contrast, enquiry models focus on students discovering knowledge or working things out for themselves. However, evidence suggests that enquiry-based learning approaches are less effective than direct teaching (Kirschner et al., 2006). One of the reasons for this is that breaking information into bite-sized chunks and teaching it directly actually reduces cognitive load. In contrast, enquiry-based approaches risk overwhelming students with large amounts of information. This can overload the working memory (Ashman, 2019a) and result in students being exposed to large amounts of extraneous information.

Direct instruction as an approach to teaching fits in with what we already know about how students learn. Mental representations or schemas develop in the brain when we learn something new. New knowledge is added and is either assimilated into the existing schema or the schema must be modified to accommodate it. During these processes of accommodation and assimilation, we link new knowledge to existing knowledge. For learning to make sense, knowledge must be introduced sequentially in smaller components. When we learn new information, new neural connections form in the brain. These form links with existing neural structures, resulting in new neural pathways which facilitate retrieval. Through direct instruction, knowledge is carefully sequenced so that it can fit into existing schemas or cause schemas to be modified. Information is delivered in small chunks to reduce cognitive load. Retrieval, including regular testing, and spaced practice are used as deliberate strategies within a direct teaching model to activate neural pathways. Through direct teaching, teachers actively support students to use the knowledge that they learn and to think critically about particular topics (Willingham, 2009).

Worked examples are used within direct teaching to reduce cognitive load. This approach is particularly effective for novice learners, although it is less effective for expert learners who learn more from solving problems independently than using worked examples (Ashman, 2019a). Initially, therefore, the teacher retains a high level of control, but the teacher gradually releases control and provides opportunities for students to work on subject content independently (Sweller et al., 2011).

MODELLING

Modelling is an important pedagogical approach within direct teaching. Students, particularly novice learners, benefit from worked examples and teacher-led models (Coombe and Martin, 2019). This reduces cognitive load. Teachers must ensure that their instructions are clear. Content should be broken down into manageable parts and demonstrated to students. The key point is that when teachers use modelling, they demonstrate to students how to perform a task rather than simply explain it to them. Responsive correction of student misconceptions is a crucial element of direct teaching and effective questioning, and observation of students' responses can support the teacher in identifying misconceptions.

Modelling is the process of making new learning explicit to pupils. It can take a variety of forms. These include:

- modelling a process on a whiteboard;
- using diagrams;
- using equipment or other objects to demonstrate something;
- combining modelling with explanations.

SOCIAL LEARNING THEORY

Modelling is a pedagogical approach which aligns with social learning theory (Bandura, 1977). Social learning, according to Bandura, involves four processes. These are shown in Figure 6.1.

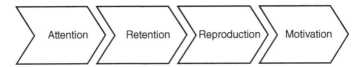

Figure 6.1   The social learning processes

We will now outline these processes in the context of modelling.

- *Attention*: the assumption of social learning theory is that attention is a key element of social learning. For students to learn from the modelling process, they must observe what the teacher is doing and saying during the process of modelling.

- *Retention*: students must then retain the information that they have been exposed to during the modelling process. If retention is weak, then this will impact on how much they learn. Retention can be supported by revisiting content and by retrieval exercises.

- *Reproduction*: social learning theory assumes that students must have opportunities to practise the subject matter that they have been exposed to during the modelling process. This will support retention. Examples include practising mathematical calculations or composing writing using structures that they have been taught during the modelling process.

- *Motivation*: Bandura (1977) argued that students need to be motivated in order for learning to take place. Extrinsic motivation can be promoted through the use of praise and tangible rewards, but being intrinsically motivated to complete a task is much more effective.

MODELLING THE STEPS

Breaking subject content down into a series of smaller steps is an effective pedagogical approach. Teachers can provide students with a list of the steps through a problem, and they can model each step systematically. This approach is particularly effective when teachers provide opportunities for students to undertake guided practice of each step after the step has been modelled. This guided practice enables students to gain support either from peers or the teacher before they are expected to work independently. Modelling the steps through a task systematically and providing opportunities for guided practice after each step supports students to develop mastery of the subject content. Teachers can use the guided practice phase to identify and address misconceptions that students may have developed before moving on to the next step.

MODELLING ABSTRACT IDEAS

Effective teachers can make abstract content meaningful to students. Abstract subject content may be content that is outside of the student's direct experience. One way of making abstract content meaningful is to use objects or other visual representations, including diagrams or videos.

SCAFFOLDiNG

Scaffolding originates from the work of Jerome Bruner (1978). He described it in the following way:

> [Scaffolding] refers to the steps taken to reduce the degrees of freedom in carrying out some task so that the student can concentrate on the difficult skill she is in the process of acquiring.
>
> (Bruner, 1978, p19)

It is very similar to Vygotsky's zone of proximal development (Vygotsky, 1978, p86), which is described as:

> the distance between the actual developmental level as determined by independent problem solving and the level of potential development as determined through problem solving under adult guidance, or in collaboration with more capable peers.

Vygotsky (1978) emphasised the importance of guidance from adults or more able peers to support students to achieve independent problem-solving. However, Bruner's (1978) concept of scaffolding is useful because it helps us to understand the role of more capable peers or adults in the process of learning. Both Vygotsky and Bruner saw learning as a social process. Scaffolding as an analogy for learning is a powerful metaphor. When a building is being erected, scaffolding supports the building in a similar way to teachers or more capable peers who support the learning of those who are working at lower stages of development. When the building is strong enough to stay in place without falling down, the scaffolding can be removed. When students have confidently mastered a skill or task under guidance from others, they no longer require the support. They can perform the skill or task independently.

Modelling is a form of scaffolding. The teacher uses modelling to guide the student. Once the student has mastered the subject content, they no longer need the model. They can effectively operate independently. The teacher must strike a fine balance. If they do not provide sufficient modelling, the student may not grasp the subject content. However, if they provide too much modelling, the student may not develop the independence required to complete the task or perform the skill without the model. The aim should be to gradually remove the modelling when it is no longer required, in the same way that the scaffolding is removed from a building. If the model is never removed, there is a danger that students will become dependent upon it.

MODELLiNG METACOGNiTiVE STRATEGiES

Metacognition has been addressed as a separate chapter in this book. It involves the skills of planning, monitoring and evaluating learning so that students achieve the best outcomes. Good learners use these metacognitive strategies all the time and they are lifelong skills.

Teachers can demonstrate metacognitive strategies by modelling how to:

- check the accuracy of mathematical calculations;
- use checklists (success criteria) to monitor the quality of work during completion of a task;
- edit work to improve it;
- self-evaluate work against the success criteria;
- use a writing frame to plan a piece of writing.

The key point is that effective learners are strategic learners. They can use the skills of planning, monitoring and evaluating to meet deadlines and goals and to improve the quality of their work. However, these skills may not be intuitive to students. Teachers need to explicitly model these strategies because they are not always intuitive.

THiNKiNG ALOUD

Thinking aloud is the process of modelling the thought processes of a learner. It enables teachers to make explicit the *thought processes* that occur when a student is approaching a task or performing a skill. It allows teachers to make explicit:

- the steps involved in completing a task or performing a skill;
- the decisions that need to be made during this process;
- the metacognitive strategies used, including checking accuracy, checking for sense and editing work.

QUESTiONiNG AND EXPLANATiONS

Teachers use questioning not only to check understanding but also to promote thinking when new subject content is being introduced. In addition, teachers use explanations to help students to understand subject content. These are modelling strategies. However, the use of visual cues to support questioning and explanations is particularly helpful during the process of modelling. Explanations can be enhanced with the use of photographs, pictures, diagrams, objects and other resources. Explanations can be enhanced by *demonstrating* a skill or process. Learning is generally more effective if dual coding is used.

ROSENSHiNE'S PRiNCiPLES OF EFFECTiVE iNSTRUCTiON

Rosenshine synthesised 40 years of research to develop ten principles of effective teaching. These can be summarised as:

1. Begin a lesson with a short review of previous learning.

2. Present new material in small steps, with student practice after each step.

3. Ask a large number of questions and check the responses of all students.

4. Provide models for problem-solving and worked examples.

5. Guide student practice.

6. Check for student understanding.

7. Obtain a high success rate.

8. Provide scaffolds for difficult tasks.

9. Require and monitor independent practice.

10. Engage students in weekly and monthly review.

(Rosenshine, 2010, 2012)

There is a strong emphasis within these principles on direct teaching through the use of modelling and guided student practice.

THE DYNAMiC MODEL OF EDUCATiONAL EFFECTiVENESS (CREEMERS AND KYRiAKiDES, 2006, 2011)

The dynamic model (Creemers and Kyriakides, 2006, 2011) identifies 21 pedagogical approaches grouped under eight headings. The model has been well-tested and is empirically sound. The strategies in the model are closely aligned with direct instruction.

	Pedagogical approaches
Orientation	(a) Providing the objectives for which a specific task/lesson/series of lessons take(s) place
	(b) Challenging students to identify the reason why an activity is taking place in the lesson
Structuring	(a) Beginning with overviews and/or review of objectives
	(b) Outlining the content to be covered and signalling transitions between lesson parts
	(c) Drawing attention to and reviewing main ideas
Questioning	(a) Raising different types of questions (i.e. process and product) at appropriate difficulty level
	(b) Giving time for students to respond
	(c) Dealing with student responses
Teacher modelling	(a) Encouraging students to use problem-solving strategies presented by the teacher or peers
	(b) Inviting students to develop strategies
	(c) Promoting the idea of modelling
Application	(a) Using seatwork or small-group tasks to provide needed practice and application opportunities
	(b) Using application tasks as starting points for the next step of teaching and learning
The classroom as a learning environment	(a) Establishing on-task behaviour through the interactions they promote (i.e. teacher–student and student–student interactions)
	(b) Dealing with classroom disorder and student competition through establishing rules, persuading students to respect them, and using the rules
Management of time	(a) Organising the classroom environment
	(b) Maximising engagement rates
Assessment	(a) Using appropriate techniques to collect data on student knowledge and skills
	(b) Analysing data to identify student needs and report the results to students and parents
	(c) Teachers evaluating their own practices

USING EXAMPLES

One of the characteristics of direct teaching is the use of examples to support concepts. According to Engelmann and Carnine (1982), students have 'the capacity to learn any quality that is exemplified through examples' (p4). Examples can bring abstract subject content to life. Many science teachers will be used to teaching the concept of 'evaporation'. However, students begin to understand this concept better when real life examples of evaporation are presented to them. Examples of this concept might include rainwater drying up in the heat and wet clothes that are left in the sun to dry. These are simple examples which bring an abstract concept to life. Teaching through examples can prevent ambiguity, but the examples chosen must show the breadth and limits of the concept being taught (Needham, 2019).

COVERTISATION

Covertisation is a strategy which encompasses the following elements:

- It initially includes *highly scripted* teacher instruction.
- Students initially follow the instructions step-by-step under teacher guidance.
- Students then follow the instructions independently.
- Eventually, the routine becomes less structured because students internalise the steps. Students do not need to work through all the steps because the learning becomes automatic.

(Rizvi, 2019)

SCAFFOLDING AND FADING

One of the key principles of direct instruction is that teachers play a key role in guiding the learning. When students are learning new knowledge, this is when they require the most support from a teacher (Cullen, 2019). This structured support is often referred to as scaffolding. Eventually, it is possible to gradually remove the support when students have reached the point where they can work independently. This is known as fading. Fading can occur when new knowledge has been internalised and automaticity has been achieved. Fading can occur within lessons, across a sequence of lessons or even across several years of a school curriculum.

FADING WITHIN LESSONS

Within lessons, students should initially be provided with a high level of support from a teacher. When students achieve mastery of the subject matter, the support is gradually decreased, and the students take greater responsibility for their own learning (Larkin, 2002). Modelling subject content through worked examples is one way of providing students with scaffolding. Initially, the teacher may demonstrate a concept using a worked example. Following this modelling, the teacher and student may then work together on further examples which are like the worked example that the teacher modelled. The teacher may decide to increase the complexity of the worked examples, although it is important not to underestimate the amount of support that students will initially require when new subject content is being introduced. Questioning should be used effectively to check students' understanding and as teachers gradually release control by moving from the 'I do' to 'we do' phases of the lesson, the teacher will introduce strategies to maximise student engagement. Cullen (2019) argues that fading should be planned into every lesson so that students have opportunities to independently work on the subject content. According to Cullen, 'every learning sequence should culminate in a moment of fading that allows pupils to put their learning into practice, as well as consolidate past learning' (p93). Fading is likely to be less successful if students are working independently on more complex content than the content that the teacher has modelled.

FADiNG ACROSS UNiTS OF WORK

Regular low-stakes testing during a unit of work supports retrieval and transfer of information to the long-term memory (Goldstein, 2011). Regular low-stakes weekly tests on essential knowledge and short quizzes in lessons will support students to learn subject content and are often more effective than re-teaching content. However, they also provide valuable information to the teacher regarding whether information is being committed to the long-term memory. Teachers can then make decisions about whether to fade in (providing additional support) or fade out (reducing support and increasing student independence). Knowledge organisers for each topic or unit of work are a valuable way of reminding students about the essential content that they need to learn, and these can be used to support self-testing. These organisers can also be live documents where information is added to them during a unit of work as new content is taught.

FADiNG ACROSS A WELL-DESiGNED CURRiCULUM

When students move on to study new topics, they will require increased scaffolding to support them in mastering new content. However, a well-sequenced curriculum that reflects the principles of spaced or distributed practice will provide opportunities for students to revisit subject content that they have been previously taught. At the point when topics are revisited, low-stakes testing is crucial to ascertain whether information has been retained and this will support the teacher in making decisions about whether to fade in or fade out. According to Cullen (2019), 'without a curriculum that revisits this essential knowledge and practices working with it, children are likely to struggle. A good curriculum has a clear direction, one that is driven by key knowledge and how this will be sequenced and revisited' (p89). Scaffolding should be eventually dismantled, but when scaffolding is removed too early, knowledge is not committed to the long-term memory and learners become disengaged (Cullen, 2019).

DiRECT TEACHiNG AND iNTRiNSiC MOTiVATiON

Research demonstrates that academic achievement is a predictor of intrinsic motivation (Bouffard et al., 2003; Garon-Carrier et al., 2016; Harter, 1981) rather than the other way round. Ryan and Deci (2000) identified competence as a vital factor for human motivation. Direct instruction therefore supports intrinsic motivation because it includes a variety of pedagogical approaches (connecting learning to prior learning, modelling, guided practice, mastery, etc.) that are designed to maximise achievement.

DiRECT TEACHiNG AND CURRiCULUM DESiGN

Knowledge forms the building blocks of a school curriculum, but carefully sequencing component knowledge ensures that students can connect new learning to prior learning. Forms of component knowledge logically combine to form composite knowledge, and accurate sequencing also enables discrete concepts to be taught in isolation before connections are made between different concepts. Concepts should be introduced with one or two concrete examples, steps in learning should be limited and there should be deliberate practice planned to enable students to master the subject content (Stockard et al., 2018). A well-sequenced curriculum reduces confusion and guarantees maximum understanding (Turner, 2019).

Evidence suggests that more progressive approaches to curriculum design, which favour problem-solving and skills-based approaches to learning, impair the life chances of the most disadvantaged students (Wheelahan, 2009). A subject-based curriculum that promotes cultural literacy is critically important for the most disadvantaged learners but also for wider social justice (Simons and Porter, 2015). Engelmann (1993) offers a model of direct instruction with tightly defined pedagogy which emphasises the importance of knowledge within subjects and therefore within the curriculum. Blake (2019) argues that attempts to address the tail of underachievement 'by substituting an alternative curriculum for underachieving young people may be well intentioned but are, in fact, a denial of fundamental entitlement for those young people' (p145). He continues by stating: 'For those children who are lower attaining, a structured route into knowledge seems a far surer bet than writing the map themselves.'

iN THE CLASSROOM

Teachers can apply the principles of direct instruction by:

- carefully sequencing subject content;
- breaking subject content into smaller chunks;
- modelling subject content in lessons;

- guiding students using scaffolding;

- providing opportunities for students to work independently on the subject content.

TAKE 5

- Correct sequencing of curriculum components is essential so that learning makes sense.

- Chunking information into smaller components reduces cognitive load.

- Explicit modelling is an essential component of direct instruction.

- Scaffolding and fading are essential components of direct instruction and ensure that students are confident with subject content before they work independently on it.

- If we want students to know something, we need to teach them it directly. Discovery learning is not effective.

SUMMARY

This chapter has outlined some key strategies that support direct instruction. It is important to remember that direct instruction is not the same thing as rote learning, and teachers should not associate it with dull teaching. The purpose of direct instruction is to ensure that students know and understand subject content before they are asked to work on it. We are not implying that investigative or enquiry approaches to learning are not useful. These approaches play a crucial role in developing students' disciplinary knowledge. For example, students need to learn how to work as geographers, historians or scientists. Our message is that students need to know and understand the subject content before they are asked to undertake enquiry. Enquiry plays a role not in teaching subject-related knowledge but in supporting students to apply their knowledge of the subject.

7
METACOGNITION

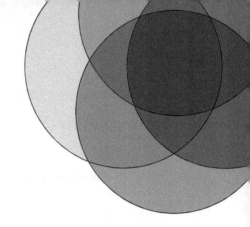

TEACHERS' STANDARDS

This chapter addresses elements of TS2, which focuses on promoting good progress and outcomes for learners.

— IN THIS CHAPTER —

This chapter introduces you to key research on metacognition. It emphasises the impact of metacognitive and self-regulation approaches in relation to student achievement and outcomes, and the key features of each approach are highlighted. Throughout the chapter, practical guidance is offered to enable you to embed metacognitive approaches within your lessons by supporting students to plan, monitor and evaluate their own learning. We emphasise that self-reflection is a critical aspect of metacognition, and the role of challenge and scaffolding is also outlined in relation to metacognition. Effective practice is illustrated through case studies.

KEY POLICY DOCUMENTATION

The *ITT Core Content Framework* states that trainee teachers must learn that:

> *Explicitly teaching students metacognitive strategies linked to subject knowledge, including how to plan, monitor and evaluate, supports independence and academic success.*

> (DfE, 2019a, p17)

KEY RESEARCH

Research findings suggest that:

- metacognition and self-regulation approaches have consistently high levels of impact, with students making an average of seven months' additional progress;

- these strategies are usually more effective when taught in collaborative groups so that learners can support each other and make their thinking explicit through discussion;

- the potential impact of these approaches is high but can be difficult to achieve in practice, as they require students to take greater responsibility for their learning and develop their understanding of what is required to succeed;

- the evidence indicates that teaching these strategies can be particularly effective for low achieving and older students.

(EEF, 2018)

Metacognition and self-regulation approaches have consistently high levels of impact, with students making an average of seven months' additional progress (Higgins et al., 2014). Metacognitive strategies help students think about their own learning more explicitly by teaching them specific strategies for planning, monitoring and evaluating their learning.

Studies demonstrate that metacognition and self-regulated learning are important to learning and thus raise attainment. According to Veenman et al. (2006), an adequate level of metacognition may compensate for students' cognitive limitations. Research demonstrates that students who are better able to delay gratification in favour of studying are also better at planning and regulating learning activities, and vice versa (Bembenutty and Karabenick, 2004).

A MODEL OF METACOGNITION

The metacognitive learner broadly follows the cycle shown in Figure 7.1.

Metacognitive practices have been shown to improve academic achievement across a range of ages, cognitive abilities and learning domains. It is therefore important that the following aspects of metacognition are used to inform and support planning and delivery:

- metacognitive knowledge (the learner's knowledge of their own strengths and weaknesses);

- metacognitive regulation (how learners monitor and control their cognitive processes). For example, realising that the strategy they are using to solve a mathematical problem is not working and then using an alternative approach;

- metacognitive practices (helping learners to plan, monitor and evaluate their own progress and take control of their learning).

(Cambridge Assessment, 2019)

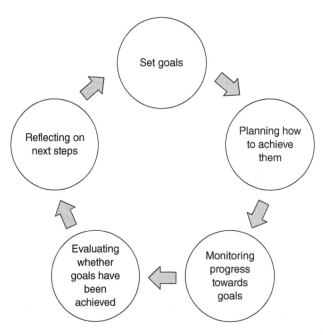

Figure 7.1   The metacognitive cycle

METACOGNiTiON

Metacognition is the process of 'thinking about one's own thinking' (Georghiades, 2004). It facilitates a deeper conceptual understanding of content and more strategic learning. Students who have good metacognitive skills can effectively monitor their own learning, regulate their own behaviour, set themselves goals, monitor their own achievement towards these and evaluate their own progress.

> *Metacognition ... is specifically about the ways learners can monitor and purposefully direct their learning, for example by deciding that a particular strategy for memorisation is likely to be successful, monitor whether it has indeed been successful, and then deliberately change (or not change) their memorisation method based on that evidence.*

(Muijs and Bokhove, 2020, p5)

Some studies consider self-regulation to be a part of metacognition, while others see metacognition as a part of self-regulation (Veenman et al., 2006). In recent years, however, the latter view has largely prevailed (Muijs and Bokhove, 2020), so for clarity, it is this view that we will follow in this chapter. Research has found that students who employ metacognitive strategies, including self-regulated learning and goal setting, are more able to engage in cognitive processes, remember information and have greater capacity for learning (Farrington et al., 2012).

Teachers can model metacognitive strategies by modelling aloud their own thinking, particularly when they explain new subject content to students. Metacognitive abilities also can enhance motivation (Cantor et al., 2019) because students are aware of their own goals, their strengths and weaknesses and can evaluate their own learning in relation to their goals.

According to the Education Endowment Foundation:

> *Metacognition and self-regulation approaches aim to help pupils think about their own learning more explicitly, often by teaching them specific strategies for planning, monitoring and evaluating their learning. Interventions are usually designed to give pupils a repertoire of strategies to choose from and the skills to select the most suitable strategy for a given learning task.*
>
> (EEF, 2018)

Metacognition consists of different components. A distinction can be made between metacognitive knowledge and metacognitive skills (Veenman et al., 2006). Metacognitive knowledge is what a learner *knows* about the way they learn or their knowledge of how they can complete a particular task efficiently (Muijs and Bokhove, 2020). Metacognitive skills refer to the ability to regulate their learning. Both interact with one another (Muijs and Bockhove, 2020). Students draw on their metacognitive knowledge to regulate their progress through a task in a systematic manner (Karably and Zabrucky, 2009). Metacognitive knowledge includes knowledge about oneself as a learner and also about the factors that influence one's performance. Metacognitive skills include planning, monitoring and evaluation. There is some evidence that indicates that metacognitive knowledge and skill is dependent on gender and socioeconomic background, advantaging females and students from culturally rich environments (Leutwyler and Maag Merki, 2009). Studies which have explored gender and self-regulation have shown that girls have better self-regulation than boys, and this finding is consistent across age phases and countries (Blankson et al., 2016; Daniel et al., 2016; King and McInerney, 2016; Koli-Vehovec and Bajšanski, 2006). These findings highlight the importance of explicitly teaching strategies for self-regulation (Muijs and Bokhove, 2020).

SELF-REGULATiON

Self-regulated learners:

> *are proactive in their efforts to learn because they are aware of their strengths and limitations and because they are guided by personally set goals and task related strategies, such as using an arithmetic addition strategy to check the accuracy of solutions to subtraction problems. These learners monitor their behaviour in terms of their goals and self-reflect on their increasing effectiveness. This enhances their self-satisfaction and motivation to continue to improve their methods of learning.*
>
> (Zimmerman, 2010, pp65–6)

Essentially, self-regulation is about the extent to which students are aware of their strengths and weaknesses and the strategies they use to learn. The concept of self-regulated learning is based on the premise that students should take responsibility for their own learning and should play an active role in the learning process (Zimmerman, 2010). It is a cyclical process which includes three phases:

1. the forethought phase (processes that precede the learning task);

2. the performance phase (processes during the learning task);

3. self-reflection phase (processes after the learning task).

(Muijs and Bokhove, 2020)

Self-regulated learners use feedback from previous learning tasks and attempt to make adjustments to future tasks (Zimmerman, 2000). Dinsmore et al. (2008) conceptualise self-regulation into three areas of psychological functioning: cognition, metacognition and motivation. Self-regulation in learning involves cognition, metacognition and motivation.

- *Cognition* refers to the mental process involved in knowing and understanding a subject and the ability to grasp subject-specific skills. Cognitive strategies include skills like memorisation techniques or subject-specific strategies.

- *Metacognition* is about the ways that students monitor and purposefully direct their learning, for example, the skills of planning, monitoring and evaluating their learning and making adaptations to improve on their performance. Metacognitive strategies enable students to monitor or control their cognition.

- *Motivation* relates to their willingness to engage their metacognitive and cognitive skills. Motivational strategies include investing effort and perseverance into a task and convincing oneself that a task needs to be completed. Motivation is influenced by motivational beliefs about oneself related to a task, for example, self-efficacy beliefs, interest or emotional reactions to oneself and the task (Boekaerts, 1999).

Self-regulated learners can motivate themselves to engage in learning and develop strategies to improve their learning. Self-regulated learners are:

- proactive in their efforts to learn;

- aware of their own strengths and weaknesses;

- good at setting their own goals to enhance their learning;

- able to check the accuracy of their work;

- able to monitor their progress towards their goals;

- able to self-reflect on their learning;

- motivated to continue to improve.

(Zimmerman, 2010)

PLANNiNG LEARNiNG

Effective learners can plan their learning by breaking down tasks into smaller parts. They can order these parts into a logical sequence so that they know what steps to complete in a clear order. They can set themselves goals so that they know what they want to achieve within a specific timescale. Providing students with templates is a useful strategy to support them in organising their thinking. Graphic organisers can also support students to think carefully about the organisation of their work. For example, templates can be used to support students in planning how to write reports across a range of subjects. The template can support them to plan the subject-specific vocabulary that needs to be included in the report, the structure of the report and the organisation of key information in the report.

MONiTORiNG LEARNiNG

Effective learners can monitor their own learning. The process of monitoring learning is ongoing and takes places during a task. Students with good metacognitive skills can identify whether they are achieving their intended goals, whether their work is good enough or whether they need to adapt it during the process of completing a task. This process of monitoring helps students to improve the quality of their work so that they achieve their goals.

One strategy for supporting learners to monitor their learning is to teach them to check their work during a task. This works particularly well in mathematics. Students can be taught strategies to check the accuracy of a mathematical calculation by using an inverse calculation, for example. In this way, students can use different calculation strategies to check their answers to mathematical problems. Another strategy is to provide students with a list of clear steps through a mathematical problem. Students follow the steps sequentially to complete the problem and then work through them again to check the accuracy of their answers. In English, teachers can provide students with checklists which identify the aspects of grammar, sentence structure, vocabulary and punctuation that must be present in a piece of writing. Students can then use the checklist during the writing task to make sure that they are including all the required features. If students start to monitor their learning during a task, this will help them to identify how to improve their work before the work is completed.

EVALUATING LEARNING

Students with good metacognitive skills can evaluate their work. Teachers can support this process of evaluation using a range of pedagogical approaches. These might include:

- providing students with clear success criteria to support evaluation;

- asking students to self-assess their work against the success criteria;

- sharing models of good work with the class and asking them to evaluate their work against these;

- introducing peer assessment;

- asking students to identify what aspects of their work are good and to also identify one aspect for improvement;

- modelling correct or good responses on the screen/board and asking students to evaluate their work in relation to the model;

- asking students to reflect on the learning process, for example, how well they work as part of a team;

- meeting students once every half term to engage them in reflecting on their strengths and weaknesses.

STRUCTURED REFLECTION

Providing opportunities for students to reflect on their work and themselves as learners is a critical aspect of metacognition. Students can be supported in this process by providing them with a set of questions or prompts that helps to structure their reflections. Students need to understand that reflection is a key component of effective learning and that effective learners are always seeking ways to improve their learning. Other strategies for facilitating reflection include students:

- writing a reflective comment at the end of a piece of work;

- reflecting on three things that they have achieved in their learning during a particular week and one thing that they want to improve on in the following week;

- keeping a reflective diary which includes evidence of their achievements, for example, through photographs and written reflections, over the duration of a year.

MODELLING THINKING ALOUD

If we want students to be authors, historians or mathematicians, for example, they need to understand how these people think. One way of helping students to start thinking as authors, historians, mathematicians is to model the process of thinking aloud. Teachers can do this during the process of modelling subject-specific content. If a teacher is modelling composition in writing, for example, it is important to support students to consider their audience. In other words, students need to understand how writers use specific features in their writing to create impact on the reader. So, let us imagine you are modelling a creative piece of writing. You might start writing the first few lines, but as you do this, you also verbalise your own thought processes. For example, you might say the following as you are writing:

- 'I need an adjective to go in front of this noun to give the reader some detail.'

- 'I am going to change this word for a better word because it gives the reader more information.'

- 'I want to include some dialogue to keep the reader engaged.'

- 'I am going to go back through this writing and change some words to make it more powerful.'

- 'I've used this word, but it's boring. Can we think of a better word?'

This strategy of thinking aloud makes explicit to students the type of thinking that you want them to demonstrate in their own work. It is a strategy which helps students to monitor and edit their work as they complete a task. This is exactly the way you want your students to complete a task. Consider now how this approach might be used in other subjects.

ADDING IN DELIBERATE DIFFICULTY

The tasks that you set the students should neither be too easy nor too hard. If they are too easy, then there is no cognitive demand. If they are too complex and involve too many steps, the cognitive load might be too great. Aim to pitch the learning at a level above the level that the student is operating at. The level should be appropriate and achievable for the student with the support of the teacher. The following process is a useful way of thinking about lesson structure:

- activate prior learning;

- model the new learning;

- introduce guided learning – this is where you support the students to complete the task, or they support each other to complete it;

- implement independent learning;

- check throughout the lesson and at the end of the lesson that they have understood.

REMOVING THE SCAFFOLDING

Providing students with scaffolding can support them to reach a higher level of development. Scaffolds can take many forms including adult support, prompts, cues and templates. If students rely on these scaffolds for too long, there is a danger that they become dependent on them and they can restrict their independence. It is therefore important to gradually remove the scaffolds so that students can achieve independence in learning. This is called fading.

METACOGNITIVE TALK IN THE CLASSROOM

Metacognitive classroom talk is talk that promotes learning. Alexander (2017) emphasises the importance of dialogic teaching. This strategy emphasises classroom dialogue through which students learn to reason, discuss, argue and explain. According to Alexander (2017), the most effective classroom talk strategies for developing metacognitive skills are *learning talk* and *teaching talk*.

- Learning talk includes narrating, questioning and discussing.

- Teaching talk includes instruction, exposition and dialogue.

Alexander (2017) argues that both discussion and dialogue are the most potent and the least common in classrooms and therefore need to be given much greater prominence.

IN THE CLASSROOM

Teachers can develop students' metacognitive knowledge by developing independent projects which require them to:

- set goals;

- plan the milestones to be achieved through a project;

- carry out an investigation or independent research;

- monitor their progress towards the milestones;

- evaluate their learning.

TAKE 5

- Ask students to set themselves goals so that they know what they want to achieve within a specific timescale.

- Encourage students to check the accuracy of their work, for example, re-working through a series of steps to check to see if their answers are correct.

- Provide students with clear success criteria to support self-reflection and evaluation.

- Model the process of thinking to help students to start thinking as authors, historians and mathematicians.

- Gradually remove scaffolds to promote students' independence in learning.

(DfE, 2019b)

SUMMARY

This chapter has outlined the metacognitive process. It has emphasised the importance of students taking control of their own learning through setting goals, monitoring and evaluating their learning and making adjustments so that they achieve their desired goals. Independent projects provide valuable opportunities for students to develop metacognitive skills, but it is essential that students have been taught the subject knowledge prior to carrying out enquiries. Developing metacognitive skills within direct instruction (for example, self-checking a strategy) should also be encouraged and teachers can explicitly model this.

8
SUBJECT KNOWLEDGE

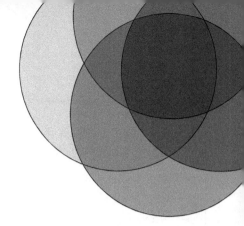

TEACHERS' STANDARDS

This chapter addresses TS3, which focuses on subject knowledge.

IN THIS CHAPTER

This chapter outlines the role of subject knowledge in teaching and the different types of subject knowledge that teachers need to promote in students. We focus on substantive and disciplinary knowledge, but we also introduce other terms, including content knowledge, pedagogical knowledge and pedagogical content knowledge. There are overlaps between these terms. It goes without saying that teachers need to have good subject knowledge. Without good subject knowledge, it is impossible to explain subject content clearly and to address students' subject-specific misconceptions. However, when good subject knowledge is combined with good pedagogical content knowledge (knowledge of effective pedagogical approaches within subjects), this maximises learning gains and increases the likelihood that students will remember the knowledge that they are being taught.

KEY POLICY DOCUMENTATION

The *ITT Core Content Framework* states that trainees must learn that:

- secure subject knowledge helps teachers to motivate pupils and teach effectively;

- ensuring pupils master foundational concepts and knowledge before moving on is likely to build pupils' confidence and help them succeed;

- in order for pupils to think critically, they must have a secure understanding of knowledge within the subject area they are being asked to think critically about.

(DfE, 2019a, pp13–14)

KEY RESEARCH

- Research on teachers' subject knowledge has yielded mixed results, though the strongest studies tend to show the strongest relationship between subject knowledge and attainment.

- Teachers' subject knowledge is not necessarily linearly related to pupil attainment. It is not the case that more teacher knowledge is in itself directly related to more pupil learning. However, there is some evidence that teachers with greater content knowledge have higher levels of pedagogical content knowledge, which itself leads to greater attention to cognitive activation (developing pupils' conceptual knowledge through, for example, summarising and questioning strategies) in their teaching.

(Ofsted, 2019, pp11–12)

According to Coe et al. (2014, p2):

The most effective teachers have deep knowledge of the subjects they teach, and when teachers' knowledge falls below a certain level it is a significant impediment to students' learning. As well as a strong understanding of the material being taught, teachers must also understand the ways students think about the content, be able to evaluate the thinking behind students' own methods and identify students' common misconceptions.

WHY IS SUBJECT KNOWLEDGE IMPORTANT?

Subject knowledge includes subject-specific facts, laws and principles. It is essential for helping students to understand subjects. Ofsted (2019) states that, 'If curriculum lies at the heart of education, and subject lies at the heart of curriculum, then it follows that teachers need solid knowledge and understanding of the subject(s) they teach. As well as this, they need to know how to teach that subject, and, more generally, how to teach' (p10). Ofsted categorises subject knowledge into content knowledge, pedagogical knowledge and pedagogical content knowledge.

- *Content knowledge* is teachers' knowledge of the subject they are teaching.

- *Pedagogical knowledge* is teachers' knowledge of effective teaching methods.

- *Pedagogical content knowledge* is teachers' knowledge of how to teach the subject or topic.

(Ofsted, 2019, p10)

When teachers have good subject knowledge, they can explain subject content with clarity, they can answer students' questions and they can ensure that students' knowledge of that content deepens over time. Teachers with subject expertise are the best people to teach the subject curriculum. These teachers will ideally have studied the subject at a high level, ideally degree level, and they will have a passion for their subject. Of course, it is not uncommon for secondary teachers to teach several subjects. This is not ideal, but it can work effectively if teachers are prepared to invest time into learning the subject content at a deep level. Teachers with strong subject knowledge motivate and enthuse their learners. They can quickly identify subject-specific misconceptions and they can address these effectively in lessons.

Strong content knowledge is essential so that teachers can explain and model subject content, including subject concepts, laws, principles and facts. Strong pedagogical content knowledge enables teachers to break subject content down into chunks, to sequence the learning, to use modelling, interleaving, spaced and retrieval practices to ensure that students develop deep knowledge and strong understanding, enabling them to work with the subject content. Strong knowledge of these practices also supports students to transfer information from their working memory into their long-term memory.

Ideally, teachers should also be members of their subject communities. This will support them to engage in debates about the subject, to collaborate and share ideas with other teachers and to engage with the latest research in their subject. Subject networks provide many professional development opportunities, and these are increasingly being held online to facilitate access and to reduce costs. School leaders can support subject knowledge development by supporting teachers to attend subject conferences or to participate in research with university academics. These opportunities help teachers to keep abreast of the latest developments within their subject. However, there is no reason why students should not also participate in these subject communities. Schools need to consider how they might facilitate opportunities for students to participate in both subject networks and attend universities to participate in lectures, seminars and workshops led by university academics. Material that is produced by the subject association can be shared with students. Many subject organisations produce a professional journal which may include opinion pieces and research papers. Teachers can use these to support discussion and debate in lessons. Many subject organisations also have websites which include blogs that students can read and discuss. As subject experts, we do not just study the subject in isolation. We network with other people with shared interests, we participate in debates, and we collaborate on research. There is no reason why students in school should be excluded from any of these learning opportunities.

Strong content knowledge is essential. Without this, teachers cannot deepen students' knowledge. However, all teachers know that content knowledge alone is not enough. Teachers need to know how to teach a subject. They need to know how to bring content to life, when to scaffold students' learning and when to use fading, and they need to know how to make learning stick. They need to know how to assess the quality of their subject curriculum, not by examination or test results, but by determining how much of the subject content their students know. Pedagogical content knowledge is therefore a critical component of being an effective subject teacher in secondary schools.

We all remember a teacher at school who had brilliant subject knowledge but could not explain the subject content clearly. We have all had a teacher who went through the material so quickly that none of the content was understood. We all remember those teachers who lost patience when we could not grasp the subject content of the lesson or the teacher who did not support us to understand our misconceptions. Knowledge of pedagogy is vital, but it is not enough by itself. Christine Counsell (2020) argues that we should not use evidence of effective pedagogical approaches in lessons as a proxy for a quality curriculum. We cannot assume that when a teacher makes a deliberate choice to use retrieval, interleaving or distributed practice within their lessons, the subject curriculum is high quality. It can only be high quality if the students know more, and their knowledge of the subject is deepening. The content knowledge alone is also not enough, particularly when teachers do not use strategies to ensure that students understand the content or strategies to make the learning stick. We need both content and pedagogical knowledge to promote learning, and this is why pedagogical content knowledge is optimal.

Teachers with strong pedagogical content knowledge understand the importance of deliberate, explicit, direct teaching. They understand that content is best introduced in small chunks, and they know that this content needs to be modelled to students and explained clearly. They recognise the need to initially guide student practice by providing scaffolding before asking students to work with the subject content individually. They know to continually check on students' learning and to ensure a high success rate from their students (Rosenshine, 2012, suggests that the optimum success rate for student achievement is 80 per cent). All these strategies are informed by Rosenshine's principles of effective instruction. They are important because they ensure that students have strong knowledge of the underpinning subject content, concepts, facts, laws and principles. Teachers with strong subject knowledge also recognise the need to teach the substantive content to students before students engage in problem-solving activities or investigative work. Students get better at mathematics by learning the underpinning mathematical principles and not by doing problem-solving activities. Students learn more from science investigations when they know and understand the scientific concepts and knowledge which underpin the investigation. If we don't teach the subject content first, then we risk students developing inaccurate knowledge, forming the wrong conclusion and experiencing a high level of cognitive load.

SUBSTANTIVE KNOWLEDGE

Content knowledge is also known as substantive knowledge. Substantive knowledge is the knowledge of the concepts, laws, theories and models within the subject.

DISCIPLINARY KNOWLEDGE

Disciplinary knowledge is the knowledge of how to work within a subject. In history, this means the knowledge of how to work as a historian. In science, it means the knowledge of how scientists work scientifically.

ADDRESSING MISCONCEPTIONS

Students may develop misconceptions in specific aspects of subject content. Your role as a teacher is to unpick these misconceptions, explain to them why these have developed and support them to develop accurate knowledge and understanding.

The best way of addressing misconceptions is to research possible misconceptions that students may develop when you are planning lessons. This will then enable you to explicitly highlight these common misconceptions in your lesson and teach students how to avoid developing them in the first place.

Understanding common misconceptions within a subject and supporting students to overcome them requires you to have strong subject knowledge. You will also need to ensure that you do not accidentally teach the students misconceptions (unless you are trying to draw their attention to them) so that they do not adopt them!

You will need to address misconceptions at various stages in a lesson. These include:

- when students answer questions and demonstrate misconceptions through their answers;
- when students are working on a task and you notice them developing misconceptions;
- when you observe students' responses to an assessment for learning task and notice that they have developed misconceptions.

BEING A SUBJECT EXPERT

Trainee teachers should:

- engage in professional discussions with colleagues in their own department;
- observe other teachers;
- join subject associations, for example, the Geographical Association or Historical Association;
- keep up to date with the latest research in the subject;
- join online communities of teachers.

PROMOTiNG HiGH STANDARDS OF LiTERACY

All teachers are teachers of literacy. You should therefore model accurate spelling, grammar and sentence structure when you are modelling text for students. It is good practice to have subject-specific vocabulary on display in lessons. It is also good practice to model written responses on the board in front of the students. Whilst you are model writing, you should articulate your thought processes to the students. This makes visible to students the thought processes you are experiencing as you are constructing the text. You want them to adopt the same thinking when they are writing, so if they see you doing this, they will be more likely to follow your example. Articulating your thought processes can also be used in other subjects, for example, in history when you are examining a historical source.

iN THE CLASSROOM

Teachers can help students to feel part of a subject community through developing partnerships with local universities. Students can participate in taster days and listen to lecturers and professors who can introduce them to exciting subject content. Teachers can also talk to students about subject associations and their own links with these organisations. Teachers can introduce students to the latest research and thinking within their subjects. This will help students to recognise that knowledge is not fixed but constantly evolving and often partial. Students can then begin to understand that our knowledge of subjects is constantly developing as a result of new research and thinking.

TAKE 5

- Good subject knowledge is a pre-requisite for effective teaching. Teachers without good subject knowledge cannot teach well.

- Good content knowledge ensures that teachers can explain subject content well.

- Good content knowledge enables teachers to address subject-specific misconceptions.

- Pedagogical content knowledge is the combination of content knowledge and pedagogical knowledge.

- Pedagogical content knowledge enables teachers to draw on evidence-based pedagogical approaches which maximise learning within the subject.

SUMMARY

This chapter has explained the distinction between different types of subject knowledge. One way of enhancing teachers' subject knowledge is for mentors in school to focus on providing trainee teachers and early career teachers with high-quality, subject-specific feedback. Teachers and trainees cannot be expected to know everything, and it is inevitable that their subject knowledge will be developed throughout their teaching careers. Teachers who keep up to date with their subjects through reading research or joining subject associations are in a stronger position because these activities and engagements will improve their subject knowledge. We also want students to view themselves as members of a subject community. Teachers should therefore consider ways of facilitating this through involving external subject experts in delivering lessons, developing partnerships with universities and introducing students to material from subject associations.

9
ADAPTIVE TEACHING

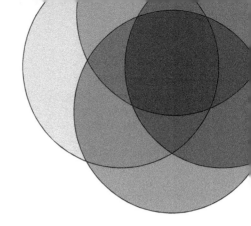

TEACHERS' STANDARDS

This chapter addresses TS5, which focuses on adapting teaching to respond to the strengths and needs of all pupils.

IN THIS CHAPTER

This chapter unpacks the term 'adaptive teaching'. Adaptive teaching is not the same thing as differentiation. Differentiation often involves setting different tasks for specific students. Too often, students with EAL or those with SEND are set tasks which are cognitively less demanding. This results in these students achieving less than their peers and in widening the ability gap between different groups of students. Adaptive teaching is both a mindset and a practice. It requires teachers to raise their expectations of what learners can achieve and it does not place an artificial ceiling on what students can achieve.

KEY POLICY DOCUMENTATION

The *ITT Core Content Framework* states that trainees must learn that:

> *Adapting teaching in a responsive way, including by providing targeted support to pupils who are struggling, is likely to increase pupil success.*
>
> (DfE, 2019a, p20)

WHAT DO WE UNDERSTAND BY ADAPTIVE TEACHING?

Adaptive teaching is not the same thing as differentiation. When teachers use differentiated instruction, they respond to variation in students' needs using a range of approaches. These might include:

- setting different learning tasks for students with differing levels of attainment;

- identifying different learning outcomes for specific students;

- providing separate instruction/teaching for children with varying levels of attainment, for example, using in-class ability groups or teaching students in different sets;

- providing different curricula for students at varying levels of attainment.

Although these approaches are well-meaning, they often place a limit on what students can achieve. Often this results in children with SEND or those with EAL being placed in lower ability groups, given tasks which are less cognitively demanding and being subjected to lower teacher expectations. The result of this is that some learners do not achieve good outcomes. The Code of Practice for Special Educational Needs and Disabilities (DfE/DoH, 2015) emphasises the need to improve outcomes for children with SEND. Far too many do not achieve good attainment and this impacts on their ability to secure good long-term outcomes, including accessing further and higher education, employment or training and independent living. Differentiated instruction is particularly responsible for this. By setting different learning outcomes for different groups of students, teachers create an artificial ceiling which limits their achievement. These practices, which fall under the umbrella of differentiation, serve to widen the ability gap. To reduce or close the ability gap, we need to change our mindset.

Adaptive teaching is a process but also a mindset. It requires teachers to believe that all students can achieve. It requires teachers to ensure that subject content is challenging for all students, and it is dependent on teachers having high expectations of all learners. When expectations are low, students will underachieve in relation to their potential. When expectations are high, students will rise to the challenge and often surprise us.

As a process, adaptive teaching is not the same as differentiation. It does not place an artificial ceiling on what students can achieve through exposing them to teaching and tasks that are less cognitively demanding, which is the case with differentiation. First and foremost, it requires teachers to consider how they might adapt or modify teaching and tasks for individuals or groups of learners to enable them to achieve. The default thinking that the teacher needs to go through when practising adaptive teaching is to consider how a task might be modified to enable access, participation and achievement. This is not meant to imply that students always need to do the same task or work towards the same learning outcomes. It is not meant to imply that all students must demonstrate the same level of achievement at a specific point in time. However, what adaptive teaching is intended to do is to demonstrate that teaching and tasks *can* often be adapted to enable students to achieve the same learning outcomes that their peers are achieving. It is a practice which ensures equity and equality of opportunity – it is a leveller.

Examples of adaptive strategies include:

- breaking a task down into small components;

- providing concrete representations of abstract concepts;

- providing access to technology to support learning, for example, using a word-processing package or using an electronic spell checker to support a writing task reduces cognitive load for students with dyslexia;

- providing students with additional support to enable them to complete the same task or understand the same content that their peers are working on;

- providing students with alternative ways of recording their learning other than using the written word;

- using dual coding so that written or auditory information is supported by visual information.

This is not an exhaustive list. However, there is an important point that we need to make. The strategies listed above, particularly the first one, are beneficial to all students. All students benefit when learning is broken down into small components, not just those with SEND or those who have EAL. This demonstrates that all students need access to high-quality inclusive teaching that is informed by the latest educational research. Students with SEND or EAL do not necessarily need different pedagogical approaches. In fact, all students benefit from some of the pedagogical approaches that are listed above and those that are mentioned subsequently in this chapter. Adaptive teaching therefore embraces the principles of equity and equality and ensures that students can achieve the best possible learning outcomes for them.

KEY RESEARCH

According to Davis and Florian (2004), there is little evidence to support the use of distinctive teaching approaches for students with specific learning difficulties, although responding to individual differences is crucial. In-class differentiation, using different tasks for specific students or different resources, has generally not been shown to have much impact on pupils' attainment (Ofsted, 2019). In Scheerens and Bosker's meta-analysis of school effectiveness research (1997), differentiation showed a null or a very weak relationship with students' outcomes. Similarly, Hattie (2009) found the effect of differentiation to be among the weakest in his seminal work on visible learning.

Conversely, *adapting teaching* in a responsive way, for example, by providing focused support to pupils who are not making progress, is likely to improve student outcomes. However, this type of adaptive teaching should be clearly distinguished from forms of differentiation that cause teachers to artificially create distinct tasks for different groups of pupils or to set lower expectations for specific students.

Based on what we have said so far, we are concerned about some of the phrases in the teachers' standards (DfE, 2011). TS5 focuses on the need to *adapt teaching to respond to the strengths and needs of all pupils* and this statement forms the broad heading for this group of standards. However, some of the statements within this group of standards do not reflect the principles of adaptive teaching and do not consider the research on differentiation. According to the teachers' standards, teachers must:

- know when and how to *differentiate appropriately*, using approaches which enable pupils to be taught effectively;

- have a clear understanding of the needs of all pupils, including those with special educational needs; those of high ability; those with English as an additional language; those with disabilities; and be able to use and *evaluate distinctive teaching approaches* to engage and support them.

(DfE, 2011, p11)

We have used italics to emphasise the phrases that we consider to be particularly problematic. There is a danger that these statements will encourage teacher education providers to induct students into the practices that are associated with differentiated instruction. We have already argued that differentiated instruction can limit students' overall achievement and widen the ability gap, and therefore we are concerned that these statements have not been updated following the publication of the *ITT Core Content Framework*. The statements in the CCF are better. They state that trainees must know that:

Adapting teaching in a responsive way, including by providing targeted support to pupils who are struggling, is likely to increase pupil success.

Adaptive teaching is less likely to be valuable if it causes the teacher to artificially create distinct tasks for different groups of pupils or to set lower expectations for particular pupils.

(DfE, 2019a, p20)

The focus in the CCF is much more on adaptive teaching, whereas the statements in the teachers' standards promote differentiation despite being listed under the category of 'adaptive teaching'. Ofsted has stated that:

Teachers present subject matter clearly, promoting appropriate discussion about the subject matter being taught. They check learners' understanding systematically, identify misconceptions accurately and provide clear, direct feedback. In so doing, they respond and adapt their teaching as necessary without unnecessarily elaborate or differentiated approaches.

(Ofsted, 2019, p13)

Again, we have used italics to demonstrate how the approach that Ofsted is promoting contrasts sharply with the approaches that are listed in the teachers' standards, and we therefore support the need to update the teachers' standards to reflect current thinking and research. We view adaptive teaching and differentiation as having distinct principles and distinct approaches, and therefore it is confusing to put them together in the teachers' standards.

EViDENCE-BASED APPROACHES FOR ADAPTiVE TEACHiNG

Approaches that are supported by evidence apply to all students. These include:

- direct instruction;
- spaced or distributed practice;
- interleaving;
- retrieval practice;
- dual coding;
- reducing cognitive load;
- elaboration.

(Ofsted, 2019)

These strategies are discussed in other chapters, so there is no need to present further research evidence or description in this chapter. Instead, we will focus on what these strategies might look like in practice for students with SEND.

DiRECT iNSTRUCTiON

Students with SEND or those with EAL benefit from explicit and direct instruction. This is particularly effective when content is chunked into small components and when students' initial attempts at working with the content are guided by the teacher (Ashman, 2019b). Enquiry-based learning approaches are less effective (Kirschner et al., 2006) because they result in increased cognitive load, and they leave students to work things out for themselves. Evidence demonstrates that worked examples are particularly effective for novice learners (Sweller et al., 2011) and many learners with SEND or EAL will fall into this category. Some SEND students may be operating at lower levels of cognition, and students with EAL are novices in relation to learning English. Worked examples will reduce cognitive load and provide clarity so that students understand the steps in a process or understand the standards which they are aiming to achieve. The use of guided practice within a model of direct teaching is particularly effective for students with SEND or those with EAL because it provides them with scaffolding to support them in working with the subject content. As learners develop increased levels of competence, fading can be applied as the support is gradually removed. Students will benefit from the structure provided by the framework 'I do', 'we do', 'you do', because it gradually supports them in developing mastery of the subject content.

SPACED OR DISTRIBUTED PRACTICE

The spacing effect supports students with SEND or those with EAL because, in contrast with massed or clustered practice, it provides opportunities for learners to revisit subject content. Revisiting content allows students to consolidate their learning and the in-built retrieval aspect of spaced practice facilitates the embedding of information into the long-term memory. Concepts can be revisited several times during a week or across a sequence of lessons and this helps students with SEND or EAL to master the content. Spacing over time is likely to be more effective than using spacing within lessons – this could confuse some students and it might be more effective to focus on a single aspect of content rather than introducing unrelated content into the lesson.

INTERLEAVING

The practice of interleaving should be used cautiously with students with SEND or EAL. It could lead to confusion and students might make greater progress if they have strong foundational knowledge of an aspect of content rather than if similar but slightly different content is introduced within lessons (EEF, 2021). Interleaving makes learning challenging in the short term and this may lead to student disengagement, particularly for those who already have cognition and learning needs.

RETRIEVAL PRACTICE

Retrieval practice is the practice of recalling information from the long-term memory. It is effective for all students because if information is not retrieved, it will be lost. In addition, the process of retrieving information forces learners to re-study the content and therefore this process supports learning. Students with SEND will benefit from participating in a range of low-stakes retrieval tasks, although the retrieval tasks might need to be modified to meet the needs of specific learners. Technology can be used to support learners in making true/false responses to questions, particularly for learners with communication needs.

REDUCING COGNITIVE LOAD

Reducing cognitive load benefits all learners. It frees up the working memory so that learners can work with new information. Strategies which reduce cognitive load and are supported by research (EEF, 2021) include the use of worked examples and scaffolds so that students do not need to remember everything. However, teachers also need to consider how to reduce extraneous load for students with SEND. One example of extraneous load are distractions in the classroom. Examples of distractions include sensory distractions, which include noise, temperature and visual distractions such as classroom displays. Autistic children may experience sensory sensitivities and may become distressed when exposed to some sensory information. Colourful displays can be very distracting for autistic children, and they are also distracting for neurotypical children. If we want students to focus on the subject content, it is important to reduce distractions which can result in extraneous load. This is one of the reasons why some classrooms for autistic children have bare walls and spaces for quiet study. It helps them to focus on the subject content.

WORKING WITH SCHEMAS

Schemas are mental models or frameworks that organise knowledge in the mind. When students learn something new, they start to form schemas. When new knowledge is added to existing knowledge, these initial schemas are either modified to accommodate the new knowledge or new knowledge is assimilated into an existing schema. When schemas change, learning has occurred. When students learn new information, they connect it with information that has already been stored. For learning to make sense, knowledge must be introduced sequentially in small chunks. If components of knowledge are not introduced in the right order, then students will become confused. Accurate curriculum sequencing can therefore support all students to assimilate and accommodate components of knowledge so that learning makes sense.

Learners with SEND and those with EAL therefore benefit from a highly structured teaching sequence where knowledge is introduced in the right order without missing out any essential knowledge. Students with dyslexia will benefit from highly structured reading, writing and spelling programmes that introduce the knowledge and skills in the correct order. This makes it easier for students to connect new knowledge with existing knowledge and this supports schema development and schema modification. Students with EAL will benefit from a highly structured language programme in addition to being immersed within a language-rich environment.

DUAL CODING

Dual coding is based on the principle that separate subsystems of the working memory process language (phonological loop) and visual and spatial information (visuospatial sketch pad). It is possible for both subsystems to work in tandem without increasing cognitive load because different types of information are being processed by different subsystems. An example of dual coding is the use of illustrations or diagrams to support written text. The written text is processed in the language subsystem of the working memory and the illustrations are processed in the visual subsystem – there is no conflict. However, dual coding is only effective if the illustrations serve a purpose and aid the students' understanding of the written text. Many learners with EAL benefit from the use of visual prompts that are used to support auditory or written information. This works effectively because the visual information is processed in a different subsystem of the working memory to the written/auditory information. This does not increase cognitive load. Many students with SEND will also benefit from information provided in more than one format. The different formats complement each other and support students to understand the subject content.

PRE-TEACHING

Pre-teaching concepts before the main lesson, subject knowledge or vocabulary is an effective strategy for all students but particularly for students with SEND or EAL. It reduces cognitive load because through the 'pre-teach', students have been introduced to the substantive subject knowledge that they need in the main lesson. Introducing students to key vocabulary prior to a lesson enables them to focus on the substantive knowledge (concepts, principles and ideas) during the lesson rather than having to worry about learning the vocabulary.

ELABORATION

According to Ofsted:

> Elaboration is defined as describing and explaining something learned to others in some detail. Ideally, this involves making connections among ideas and connecting the material to one's memory and experiences. It can also be useful for learners to ask themselves or each other questions that require making connections between ideas or explaining them. This can clearly be built into classroom activities.

(Ofsted, 2019, p20)

Consider how you might use this strategy within a curriculum subject so that students can understand a specific aspect of subject content.

SECOND LANGUAGE LEARNERS

Students with English as an additional language do not necessarily have special educational needs. Their difficulties in learning may arise because they are in the process of learning another language rather than due to an underlying difficulty. They will benefit from being immersed in a social and communication-rich environment. They may benefit from a structured language and communication intervention. Pre-teaching vocabulary and texts is a useful strategy to maximise their participation during lessons. Aim to support your explanations and modelling with visual cues, manipulatives and other resources. Provide concrete manipulative resources to support their learning and allow them to code switch between English and their first language if they cannot identify the word in English.

Cummins' (1980) model of bilingualism demonstrates that students will draw upon understandings from their first language in order to support them to learn an additional language. This existing understanding acts as an 'anchor' to further learning of and through additional languages (Bligh, 2014). Cummins (1980) refers to this as common underlying proficiency (CUP), which includes basic interpersonal communication skills (BICS) and cognitive academic language proficiency (CALP).

BICS refers to social and conversational language and the surface skills of listening and speaking, including observing non-verbal behaviours and reactions, voice cues and imagery. These are often learnt through playful social participation with speakers of the same language (Bligh, 2014). On the other hand, CALP relates specifically to the language of the academic classroom, where non-verbal cues are typically absent and literacy demands are much higher. This therefore includes the necessary knowledge and skills required to work academically in a classroom and the ability to think in and use language as a tool for learning (Bligh, 2014).

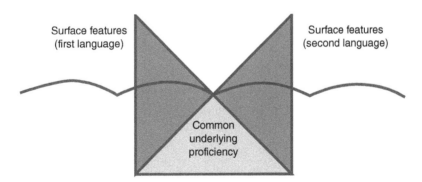

Figure 9.1   The dual iceberg model
(source: Cummins, 1980)

The model (see Figure 9.1) is represented by two icebergs that are separated above the surface of the water. The peak of each iceberg represents a language, and despite appearing visibly different, they merge into one below the surface. It is the CUP, which is found below the surface, that enables bilingual learners to function in more than one language. However, if a student is lacking CUP in one language, then it is likely that they will find it difficult to learn another.

It is therefore clear that language and communication interventions in a second language will be ineffective if a student has not met the required threshold of CUP in their first language. This has clear implications in relation to the content and structure of intervention programmes. It demonstrates that interventions must be appropriate and responsive to the needs of individual students in relation to the explicit and meaningful development of BICS and CALP. For example, offering students the opportunity to practise verbal conversations is not cognitively demanding and, as such, will support the development of BICS. This is because this activity allows students to practise conversational language and listening and speaking skills. On the other hand, scientific investigations will be cognitively demanding and promote the development of CALP. This is because scientific investigations will expose students to subject-specific vocabulary and the knowledge and skills required to work and think academically.

DEPLOYMENT OF TEACHING ASSISTANTS

Schools deploy teaching assistants to improve outcomes for students with SEND. However, research demonstrates that:

- the ineffective deployment of teaching assistants does not lead to improved student outcomes;

- students with the highest levels of SEND often make the least progress due to ineffective deployment arrangements;

- when they are well-trained and used in structured settings with high-quality support and training, teaching assistants can make a noticeable positive impact on student learning.

(Sharples et al., 2015)

IN THE CLASSROOM

Teaching assistants have more impact on students' learning if they are trained to deliver specific interventions rather than being asked to support students generally in the classroom. Impact is also maximised if teachers and teaching assistants have dedicated time to plan learning tasks.

— TAKE 5 —

- Differentiation widens the ability gap.

- Adaptive teaching requires teachers to raise their expectations of students.

- Adaptive teaching does not place an artificial limit on what learners can achieve.

- Adaptive teaching involves modifying teaching or tasks so that students can achieve their full potential.

- Learners with SEND or EAL often make the least progress because they spend the most time being supported by teaching assistants.

SUMMARY

This chapter has emphasised the importance of adapting lessons or tasks so that learners with SEND or EAL can achieve their full educational potential. We have outlined some key pedagogical approaches which will support you to adapt your teaching. We have outlined some key theories and research in this area, and we have provided some clear guidance on how to work with teaching assistants.

10
ASSESSMENT

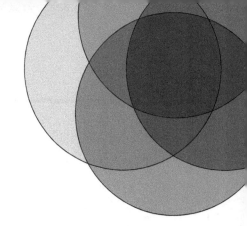

TEACHERS' STANDARDS

This chapter addresses elements of TS6, which focuses on assessment.

IN THIS CHAPTER

This chapter outlines the role of assessment in learning. It emphasises that assessment should be used to identify whether students know and understand subject content rather than using assessment for the purpose of assigning grades through high-stakes examinations. We argue that high-stakes assessments only assess a limited aspect of a subject domain. Regular formative assessment should be embedded into lessons to determine students' knowledge of the full breadth of subject content. We explore the relationship between assessment and curriculum design and the role of feedback in students' development.

KEY POLICY DOCUMENTATION

The *ITT Core Content Framework* states that trainees must learn that:

> *Effective assessment is critical to teaching because it provides teachers with information about pupils' understanding and needs.*

(DfE, 2019a, p23)

THINKING ABOUT ASSESSMENT

Dylan Wiliam (2020) draws attention to the misuse of assessment in recent years. He argues that student grades have been used to inform judgements about the quality of education that schools provide. In recent years, poor student performance data has resulted in schools failing their inspections. Consequently, schools have focused on teaching the subject content that is tested and on developing students' examination techniques to maximise student performance. The problem with this is that tests and examinations only scratch the surface of subjects. Therefore, they are not always good indicators for how well students know a subject. Wiliam (2020) argues that examination grades provide very little information about the quality of a student's education because educational attainment is influenced by the student's social background and other personal characteristics (Wiliam, 2012).

SUMMATIVE AND FORMATIVE ASSESSMENT

Wiliam (2020) emphasises that the same assessment can be used for summative or formative purposes. For example, if a student scores 50 per cent on a multiplication test, this can provide a summative judgement (the student knows 50 per cent of the multiplication facts) and it can be used formatively (the student requires further support on multiplication facts). When assessment tasks are used for summative purposes, they provide a summary of a student's achievement at a point in time. When assessment is used for formative purposes, they provide valuable information to the teacher and the student about where they are at in their learning, what they need to do next and how to get there. Wiliam (2020) is therefore keen to emphasise that there are formative and summative *uses* of assessment rather than formative or summative assessment tasks. That said, some tasks may be more suited to formative purposes and others may be more suited for summative purposes (Wiliam, 2020).

Formative assessment supports teachers to gain the information they need to close the gap between where a student is and where they need to be (Hattie and Clarke, 2019), and when done well, it dramatically improves the progress of students (Black and Wiliam, 2005). It enables teachers to check understanding, identify and address misconceptions (Ofsted, 2019) and it needs to be specific and focused (Christodoulou, 2017).

ASSESSMENT AND CURRICULUM DESIGN

Odell (2020) highlights that curriculum design and assessment are intertwined. The key is to design the curriculum by deciding the endpoint. Crucially, it is important for school leaders and heads of department to identify what knowledge all students need to know and understand. They can then work backwards from this point to plan the incremental steps that students need to move through to reach this point. Odell (2020) advises that the endpoint is determined by identifying what the highest attaining students need to know and be able to do. We then work backwards from this point to plan the incremental steps towards this point. It is then possible to design a model of assessment based on this progression model.

ASSESSiNG SUBSTANTiVE SUBJECT KNOWLEDGE

Traditional models of assessment in schools are norm-referenced. Within this model of assessment, students are ranked against each other and plotted on a bell curve. A few outliers achieve excellent or poor grades while the majority are bunched in the middle. Grade thresholds are determined after the assessments have been conducted. The problem with norm-referenced assessments is that there is an insufficient focus on what students know and 'the richness or paucity of their bodies of knowledge' (Powley, 2020, p60). An alternative approach to norm-referenced assessment is criterion-referenced assessment. In criterion-referenced models, there are clear thresholds that state what students need to know to achieve specific standards. This is a fairer model of assessment than norm-referenced assessment because the criteria can be made explicit to students. They then know what they need to know to reach a specific threshold, and the criteria can outline the rich body of knowledge that students need to learn within specific subjects.

The curriculum should expose students to powerful knowledge that provides them with cultural and linguistic capital. This is a leveller for inequality because 'everyone is entitled to a foundation of knowledge' (Young and Lambert, 2014, p16) and this is the starting point for an equal, fair and just society. Powley (2020) argues that norm-referenced assessment places the learner within a ranking system, but criterion-referencing encourages a focus on assessment of the learning, that is the substantive and disciplinary knowledge that is specific to subjects. Chief inspector for Ofsted, Amanda Spielman, stated back in 2019 that, 'we have reached the limits of using data alone as a proxy for educational quality' (Spielman, 2019). The focus on examination results has resulted in an insufficient emphasis on providing students with access to powerful knowledge – knowledge that can spark interest and enthusiasm for subjects, and that can transform life chances.

Criterion-referenced assessment requires students to know the breadth and depth of the subject content that they have been taught. Given that the optimum success rate for student achievement is 80 per cent (Rosenshine, 2012), students who achieve this have acquired fluent knowledge (Powley, 2020). They know and understand the subject content that they have been taught and have studied. Powley (2020) argues that, as educators, we are too easily satisfied with scores less than this. However, a lower score suggests that there are gaps in students' knowledge, that knowledge and understanding is not fluent, and this can impact on motivation and engagement.

Regular low-stakes testing of knowledge activates neural structures in the brain and forces retrieval. The important thing is not the grade or score that students achieve in the test, it is ascertaining what students know and what they don't know. Tom Sherrington (2017) emphasises that 'grades themselves do not actually tell us much at all about what students know or can do at a level that is actionable' (p117). Summative examinations only assess samples of the subject domain rather than the whole of the domain (Powley, 2020). Low-stakes quizzes and tests can, in contrast, assess students' knowledge of the whole subject domain. Hattie and Timperley (2007) emphasise that where assessments identify gaps in knowledge, it is more effective to re-teach that content than to provide feedback. Therefore, based on Rosenshine's 80 per cent threshold, it might be more effective to re-teach that subject content rather than spend time writing comments on students' work (Powley, 2020).

Curriculum planning should be carefully sequenced to identify component knowledge. These are bite-sized pieces of knowledge that students need to know to move onto the next step. Sequences of learning should identify these aspects of component knowledge. When students master all the components, they can then achieve the composite knowledge. This is the overall knowledge that is made up of all the components (see Figure 10.1). These are taught so that by the end of the sequence, the student knows, understands and can do the composite. It is therefore logical to assess students' knowledge of each of the components during a teaching sequence as well as assessing their mastery of the composite knowledge at the end of a teaching sequence. It is useful across an academic year to assess students' knowledge of components and composites that they have previously been taught. This will facilitate retrieval.

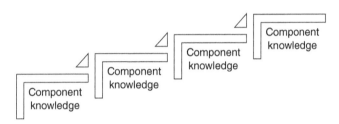

Figure 10.1   Component and composite knowledge

CONCEPTUAL UNDERSTANDING

Concepts are big ideas or principles within subjects that have an essential place within the structure of knowledge (Morris, 2009). Some concepts are abstract, and examples or concrete representations might need to be used to help students understand them. Curriculum progression models should outline curriculum progression in the following:

- *Knowledge*: the knowledge we want students to acquire.

- *Concepts*: the concepts that are integral to the subject.

- *Understanding*: the understanding that students need to demonstrate.

- *Skills*: the skills we wish them to develop.

The progression model should outline what progress looks like within a subject and it should essentially form the curriculum that students will study and the assessment framework for that subject.

SEQUENCING

If the curriculum is designed as a progression model, sequencing or stepped learning is an essential component of that model. The component parts needed to learn a particular skill essentially form the incremental steps that students work through to enable them to eventually perform the skill. Sequencing therefore plays an essential role in curriculum design, but each of the steps (components) can be assessed. The sequence of learning (progression model of curriculum design) can then be used to set targets. These targets will support the student to move on to the next step. It is therefore not possible to separate assessment and feedback from curriculum design.

SUCCESS CRITERIA

Research demonstrates that the use of clear success criteria has a significant impact on learning (Hattie and Clarke, 2019). Students should be provided with the end goal (or standard they are aiming for), and the steps that they need to take to achieve that goal should be clearly presented. One effective strategy is to deconstruct a worked example with the students. Students can use the worked example to identify the success criteria. This enables students to identify the essential components that are required to reach the end goal.

GUIDED AND DELIBERATE PRACTICE

All students need opportunities to practise. A highly skilled swimmer cannot perfect their skill if they do not practise. When we are learning to drive a car, our driving skills improve through practice. Practice is integral to effective student learning. In guided practice, the teacher supports the students to practise. This reduces the chance of students developing misconceptions (Sherrington, 2019a). Teacher guidance and support at this stage generates a high success rate which helps students to stay intrinsically motivated. Once students become confident, they can then start to practise the skill independently.

The crucial question is *what* skills to assess. Odell (2020) argues that we often focus on assessing the final skill (or the overall goal). However, it might be more productive to assess the component skills because this enables teachers to provide students with more granular feedback.

BUILDING ASSESSMENT TASKS INTO LESSONS

One assessment for learning strategy is to integrate mini assessment tasks into lessons. These tasks enable teachers to check understanding at specific stages during a lesson. They provide information to the teacher about students' understanding so that lessons can be adjusted if students have not understood what they have just been taught. If the tasks indicate that students have not understood, the teacher can then re-teach that content by breaking the content down further, re-teaching it, addressing misconceptions or by teaching it in a different way. In this way, the teacher uses the outcomes of the assessment to inform their teaching during the lesson.

Assessment for learning tasks can include quizzes, questions that students complete individually, in pairs or in groups. They are usually short tasks that are specifically planned to enable the teacher to check students' understanding before moving on to a different stage in the lesson. They can be planned:

- at the start of a lesson to check students' understanding of subject content that was taught in a previous lesson;

- after new learning has been modelled and explained;

- throughout the lesson;

- at the end of a lesson.

If the feedback from these tasks indicates that many students have not understood the subject content, the content may need to be re-taught to everyone. However, if specific students demonstrate that they have not understood the subject content, these students can be targeted individually or in a small group during the lesson so that their misconceptions can be addressed.

QUESTIONING

Research has found that the questions used by teachers are often insufficiently challenging for students (Flórez and Sammons, 2013). In addition, studies have found that the time given to elaborate on an answer is often too short (Condie et al., 2005; Gipps et al., 2005; Kellard et al., 2008; Kirton et al., 2007; Webb and Jones, 2009). Research has recommended increasing the time given for students to think of an answer (Webb and Jones, 2009) and making greater use of open questions rather than closed questions (MacPhail and Halbert, 2010) to promote higher-order thinking. Creating a positive classroom climate in which misconceptions are addressed enables students to learn from mistakes (Torrance and Pryor, 2001) and promotes learning. Specific questions should be planned to check students' understanding or to promote thinking. Questions that require students to give more detailed or multiple responses than a single correct answer are more effective at promoting thinking (MacPhail and Halbert, 2010).

SELF-ASSESSMENT

Research has demonstrated how self-assessment can promote metacognitive skills (Brookhart, 2001; Gipps et al., 2005; Stiggins and Arter, 2002). During the process of self-assessment, students learn to evaluate their work in relation to the expected outcomes. They identify what they have achieved in relation to the original goals and they suggest improvements that strengthen their work. This process of evaluating learning is critical to becoming a good learner.

The process of self-assessment should be ongoing. It should take place during the process of completing a task in addition to taking place when the task is finished. This helps students to evaluate their work as they go along and adjust it to make improvements. Self-evaluation is generally more effective if students are clear from the outset about the criteria for assessment. One way of addressing this is to provide students with a checklist so that they know what aspects to include in their work. This works particularly well in writing tasks.

PEER ASSESSMENT

Research demonstrates that students generally are more accepting of feedback from their peers rather than feedback from their teacher (Flórez and Sammons, 2013). Teachers need to carefully consider the pairings that are used during the process of peer assessment. One strategy that might be adopted is to pair students who are working at different stages of development. A decision will also need to be made about whether the pairings will be consistent across the academic year or whether different pairings will be used so that students gain feedback from other peers across the year. Students will also need to be trained in the process of peer assessment. They need to understand the purposes of peer assessment and how to give feedback. Teachers need to establish a supportive classroom climate so that all students view peer feedback as a supportive and developmental process.

FEEDBACK

Hill (2020) highlights some of the key reasons why feedback can be ineffective.

- It often focuses on the task that the student has just completed rather than helping the student to improve in future tasks.

- Students don't understand it.

- It often includes vague comments rather than actionable advice.

Hill (2020) argues that writing on a piece of work is often a highly inefficient way of providing feedback. She emphasises that whole class/group feedback is often more effective, particularly if the feedback is presented in a simple table with four sections (see Figure 10.2).

Praise	Model / exemplar
Provide examples of what students have done well	*The model can be written with the students*
Misconceptions	**Next steps**
Identify key subject misconceptions	*These should be precise and actionable, giving students an opportunity to improve their work*

Figure 10.2   Model of whole group feedback

(source: Hill, 2020, p40)

The 'next steps' box should ideally include two next steps, which can be numbered. The teacher can write the number on the student's work so that they know which next step to focus on. Highlighting misconceptions and next steps to all students is beneficial. A multiple-choice quiz can also be an effective tool to identify what needs to be re-taught.

Feedback should consider the steps shown in Figure 10.3.

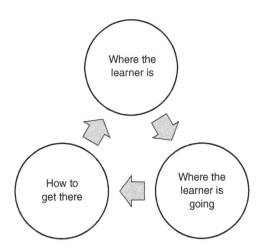

Figure 10.3   The purpose of feedback

Research from Hattie and Timperley (2007) suggests that models of feedback should address three questions:

1. Where am I going?

2. How am I going?

3. Where to next?

According to Hattie and Timperley (2007), the answers to these questions enhance learning when there is a discrepancy between what is understood and what is aimed to be understood. Feedback can increase effort, motivation or engagement to reduce this discrepancy, and/or it can increase cue searching and task processes that lead to understanding (thus reducing this discrepancy). Feedback is among the most critical influences on student learning. A major aim of the educative process is to assist in identifying these gaps ('How am I doing?' relative to 'Where am I going?') and to provide remediation in the form of alternative or other steps ('Where to next?').

Feedback comments should be specific rather than general. Comments such as 'good work' are unhelpful because this does not communicate to students why the work is good. More specific praise is beneficial, for example, *'You have used some good imperative verbs in these written instructions'*.

Good quality feedback is an essential aspect of assessment for learning (MacPhail and Halbert, 2010). Seminal research found that when students were given comment-only feedback rather than assigning marks or grades, they subsequently did better in achievement tests (Butler, 1987). Informative and descriptive feedback is more effective than simply marking students' work as correct or incorrect (Flórez and Sammons, 2013). This is because marking students' work as right or wrong can promote competition between students, which can damage the self-esteem of students who get low scores.

Feedback should provide students with guidelines not only about what is incorrect in their work, but also on what has been done correctly in relation to the initial learning goals or expectations. Explicit guidance on what they could do to improve and keep on progressing towards expectations is also essential. This feedback practice promotes greater motivation and commitment to enhancing their own learning than feedback where work is marked as either correct or incorrect and where marks are then assigned (Flórez and Sammons, 2013).

LiVE FEEDBACK

Once teachers set students off on a task, it is relatively simple to use live feedback in lessons. The teacher can select two or three pieces of work and display these on the visualiser.

The teacher can then provide feedback on the work. Students can then immediately use this feedback in the lesson to improve their work.

KEY RESEARCH

There is consistent evidence that assessment for learning increases students' achievement (Hayward and Spencer, 2010; Webb and Jones, 2009). The work of Black and Wiliam (1998) has also been influential in highlighting the benefits of assessment for learning.

> There is a body of firm evidence that formative assessment is an essential component of classroom work and that its development can raise standards of achievement. We know of no other way of raising standards for which such a strong prima facie case can be made.
>
> (Black and Wiliam, 1998, p12)

TESTING

The assumption that testing and quizzing are detrimental to learners is a myth, as evidence suggests that the use of low-stakes testing can contribute to learning in valuable ways. Research has demonstrated the importance of retrieval practice (Barenberg et al., 2018). This research shows strong evidence for the *testing effect*. This means that when students take a test shortly after studying a piece of material, they perform better on a final test than those who do not, even if no feedback is given on the initial test. This is because the process of testing knowledge forces retrieval. This evidence supports the use of frequent low-stakes testing within and between units of work. Davies (2020) suggests that formative assessment, such as multiple-choice quizzes, should be continuous and non-graded.

AUTHENTIC ASSESSMENT

There are several aspects that learners need to know.

- What stage have we reached?
- What is the final goal?
- How far are we away from the final goal?
- Are we doing well based on our own self-knowledge?
- Are we doing well based on other people's views of us?
- Are we doing well based on our previous performance?

- How well are we doing based on the performance of others?

- How challenging was the task?

(Adapted from Sherrington, 2020)

We need to know our absolute position (where we are), our distance from the goal, and we need some overall judgement about the quality of our performance. The quality judgement will be informed by the standards, but there is also a comparative element to this which relates to how other people have performed on the same assessment. Sherrington (2020) argues that students need granular assessment and granular feedback in all subjects. This is feedback which focuses on component knowledge and skills. Much granular feedback will be verbal and provided to students individually or as a whole class, but it is this type of feedback that is the most meaningful and has the greatest impact on learning (Sherrington, 2020). Authentic assessment systems provide meaningful feedback. They do not provide 'flight paths' (Sherrington, 2020): data collection points are kept to a minimum and feedback comments provide concrete actions that students should take to improve (Sherrington, 2020).

iN THE CLASSROOM

Regular quizzes, including multiple-choice tests, can be highly effective in helping teachers to quickly identify what students know. Quizzes can be used to assess the aspects of component knowledge within a unit of work. They provide teachers with valuable information during a unit of work, including whether students know and understand the subject content or whether the content needs to be re-taught, and they highlight whether teachers can move on to the next aspect of component knowledge.

TAKE 5

- Low-stakes formative assessment can be used to identify what students know and understand.

- Assessment tasks should assess the full breadth of subject content.

- High-stakes assessments can only partially determine what subject content students know and understand.

- Feedback plays a critical role in helping students realise what they know, understand and can do, and what their next steps in learning are and how they can be achieved.

- Assessment tasks should assess component knowledge, not just composite knowledge.

SUMMARY

This chapter has emphasised the positive impact that regular low-stakes formative assessment can have on students' learning. It has highlighted the importance of assessing students' knowledge across the full subject domain and the limitations of relying on high-stakes summative assessment. We have outlined the features of effective feedback and we have presented the research evidence that supports formative assessment.

11
CURRICULUM DESIGN

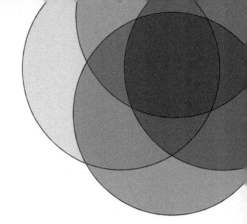

TEACHERS' STANDARDS

This chapter addresses TS2, which focuses on securing good progress and outcomes for students. We address this through curriculum design.

— IN THIS CHAPTER

This chapter addresses the concept of powerful knowledge. We highlight the importance of accurate curriculum sequencing in the process of curriculum design so that learning makes sense to students. The role of subjects in promoting cultural capital is also addressed. We argue that examination results should not be used as a proxy for curriculum quality because they do not provide a reliable indication of what students know, understand and can do in relation to subject content.

KEY POLICY DOCUMENTATION

The *ITT Core Content Framework* states that trainees must understand that:

- learning involves a lasting change in pupils' capabilities or understanding;

- where prior knowledge is weak, pupils are more likely to develop misconceptions, particularly if new ideas are introduced too quickly;

- requiring pupils to retrieve information from memory and spacing practice so that pupils revisit ideas after a gap are also likely to strengthen recall.

(DfE, 2019a, pp11–12)

These statements about how students learn have implications for curriculum design in schools. Good curriculum design should reflect some of the emerging evidence from cognitive science, including explicit and direct instruction, interleaving and distributed or spaced practice.

KEY RESEARCH

The Education Inspection Framework: Overview of Research (Ofsted, 2019) states that:

- international evidence indicates that a focus on only a few measurable outcomes has had some negative consequences for curriculum design.

- pupils from disadvantaged backgrounds are less likely to study academic subjects, including the English Baccalaureate (EBacc);

- pupil premium (PP) students are less likely to take English Baccalaureate (EBacc) subjects compared with non-PP students with similar prior attainment;

- there is evidence internationally which demonstrates that high-stakes testing has led to curriculum narrowing and curriculum content has been reduced to mirror test-related content.

(p5)

WHAT iS POWERFUL KNOWLEDGE?

An effectively designed curriculum should provide students with access to powerful knowledge. According to Professor Michael Young, 'that is the best knowledge that we have in each subject but that at least 50% of pupils in this country are denied access to' (Young, 2020, p19). This is an important point because it raises fundamental questions about equity, equality of opportunity and social justice. Young emphasises that all students, regardless of assumptions about their academic ability, have a right to acquire this knowledge.

Decisions about what is taught in the curriculum are not just matters for teachers to decide. Debates about what is taught in the curriculum have been hugely political and influenced by social background. Governments largely determine the curriculum, and in England, the roots of a knowledge-led curriculum have been firmly planted by the political right rather than the political left (Young, 2020). Students who attend fee-paying independent schools are more likely to receive a classical education, but this may not be the case for students who attend state schools. All students have a right to study classical literature and Latin, not just those who can afford to pay for it.

Sealy (2020) reminds us that high-stakes testing has, in recent years, formed the basis of a curriculum. This has limited curriculum breadth and has meant that many students do not learn the knowledge that they need to learn. The knowledge which has been tested has formed the basis of the curriculum that has been taught and this has meant that knowledge domains within subjects have only partially been covered.

Decisions about what is taught are not solely political decisions. The National Curriculum sets out the minimum expectations in relation to what students need to know, understand

and be able to do. However, schools are expected to go beyond this. School leaders decide on the intent of their curriculum. Curriculum intent forms part of the 'quality of education' judgement in the *Education Inspection Framework* (EIF) (Ofsted, 2019). Intent includes the rationale for the curriculum, which should be ambitious, and the knowledge and skills that the school wants the students to learn. Intent has become an education buzzword in recent years, but it is important. A carefully designed curriculum should be designed to give all students, including those with SEND and those who are most disadvantaged, the knowledge and cultural capital that they need to succeed in later life. The curriculum should be coherently planned and sequenced so that students develop cumulatively suffi-cient knowledge and skills. It should be ambitious for all students and ensure that students study the full curriculum.

Powerful knowledge is a contested term. What some people might consider to be powerful, others might not. However, there is some general agreement in the literature that powerful knowledge encompasses the following:

- It is not common-sense or everyday knowledge. It is specialist knowledge.

- It is challenging and it can be abstract.

- It should be taught by teachers who are experts within their subject.

- It may require access to specialist facilities, including specialist teaching rooms.

- It is critically debated within subject communities by subject experts and is sometimes contested.

- It enables students 'to hold their own in circles of power and even have a seat at the proverbial table' (Reid, 2020, p42).

(Young, 2020)

SUBJECT DOMAINS

Before teachers can become curriculum makers, they need to understand the substantive and disciplinary knowledge within their subject. We expand further on this in Chapter 8. The subject curriculum that students receive is a selection from the whole subject domain (Counsell, 2018) and teachers therefore need to make decisions about what to select. In Key Stage 4 and beyond, this is often largely determined by examination board specifications. This raises questions about who makes decisions about curriculum design, who has the power, what is included and what is missed out.

The knowledge in a subject has been described as 'a web of interconnected pieces' (Ashbee, 2020, p37). Some subjects have a vertical structure in that knowledge is linear – students need to understand one concept before they understand a different concept. Mathematics is perhaps the best example of this, but vertical structures are also evident in other subjects. The hierarchical structure of knowledge makes it relatively easy to make decisions about how to sequence the curriculum. Some subjects have a horizontal structure where knowledge is not hierarchical but is linked in some way. Examples of subjects with horizontal structures include technology, art and geography. Careful curriculum sequencing is still important in these subjects because students need to understand the connections between different aspects of knowledge within the subject.

CULTURAL CAPITAL

Pierre Bourdieu (1984) introduced the term 'cultural capital' over three decades ago. It is a word which is well known in the sociological community, but it has only recently been applied to the school curriculum. When Ofsted used the term back in 2019, many teachers and leaders did not know what the term meant, particularly if they had not studied sociology. During inspections, inspectors will evaluate the extent to which 'leaders adopt or construct a curriculum that is ambitious and designed to give learners, particularly the most disadvantaged, the knowledge and cultural capital they need to succeed in life' (Ofsted, 2019, p4).

The *School Inspection Handbook* states that cultural capital:

> is the essential knowledge that pupils need to be educated citizens, introducing them to the best that has been thought and said *and helping to engender an appreciation of human creativity and achievement.*

(Ofsted, 2021)

The text set in the non-italicised font is our own emphasis. Bourdieu identified three sources of cultural capital:

1. *objective*: cultural goods, books, works of art;

2. *embodied*: language, mannerisms, preferences;

3. *institutionalised*: qualifications, education credentials.

Cultural capital is not only provided by the curriculum, it is provided by families and communities. Children with more cultural capital tend to do better at school. This is because the education system values specific forms of knowledge developed by acquiring cultural capital. In later life, cultural capital helps individuals to network with others who share the same cultural capital, and those with greater cultural capital can access top professions, which enables them to purchase economic capital. Cultural capital is then objectified through possessions that can be purchased.

Some people possess more cultural capital than others because of their social backgrounds. Disadvantaged students are likely to know less vocabulary than those from more advantaged backgrounds. They may not have developed important cultural awareness and they may not have visited places of geographical, cultural or historical significance. They may have limited or no awareness of great literature and they may not know how to regulate their behaviour in different social contexts.

There are questions you might ask: Why is all this important? Why do students need to know about the *Magna Carta*? Why do they need to know about work of great composers? Why do they need to know about the cultures and empires of Mali, Songhai and Benin and the great kings and queens? Why do they need to know the works of Jane Austen and Charles Dickens? How will all this abstract 'stuff' help them in life, and is it even relevant to their lives? These are questions that teachers might well consider. Some might argue that one of the drivers for this push on cultural capital is to weaken the working class through providing young people with the knowledge that they will need to achieve social mobility. Others might argue that the emphasis on middle-class values is a way of denouncing working-class values and that it is a strategy for imposing middle-class values on working-class children.

These are important questions and there are multiple answers. Firstly, cultural capital enables individuals to access opportunities that they might otherwise be excluded from. If we want our students to access the top jobs, then more than a sprinkling of cultural capital will help to facilitate that. The purpose of education, though, is not just to gain employment. Secondly, all children have a right to access this knowledge simply because, for some at least, it will ignite a fire within them that will never be extinguished. This is the most powerful argument for making a case for a curriculum that embeds cultural capital and far exceeds any argument about social mobility or employment outcomes. Thirdly, some children have access to this knowledge through their families, their connections and through their communities, but others do not. This raises questions of equity, rights and social justice. There is no reason why students from less advantaged backgrounds should not also have access to this knowledge and there is no reason to assume that they will find it irrelevant or not interesting. Some of the curriculum content is challenging, but as Aurora Reid points out, it is the teacher's job to bring it alive (Reid, 2020). Providing all children with cultural capital through the curriculum is a leveller. It reduces the advantageous effects of social backgrounds and ensures equality of opportunity.

The problem with cultural capital is that there is a heavy emphasis on teaching students about the achievements of dead, white, able-bodied men. There is an urgent need to decolonise the curriculum. Students also need to learn about the significant achievements of people of colour, those who are LGBTQ+ or gender diverse and the achievements of women. They need to learn about the achievements of disabled people and about different societies, cultures and histories rather than a relentless focus on British history. It is not enough for students to learn about Britain in the Middle Ages, the effect of the Roman invasion on Britain, British parliamentary democracy, the British Empire or the role of Britain in the two world wars. They deserve far more than this. Students are global citizens and they need a global curriculum that helps them to understand the global community in which they live.

In developing a curriculum that embeds cultural capital, it is essential that students learn about the history of the working classes and their contribution to the infrastructure of modern society. Our great waterways and architectural structures were built by the working classes. Students need to know not only about famous musicians, artists, scientists, authors and mathematicians but also about the contribution of miners to the Industrial Revolution and beyond. Students cannot learn everything in a curriculum, but teachers now have the power to decide what to include and what to exclude. Decolonising and diversifying the curriculum is a good starting point because this reduces structural inequality.

CURRiCULUM COHERENCE AND SEQUENCiNG

Neil Almond (2020) offers a sound piece of advice for teachers who are working on curriculum design:

> there needs to be pause for thought as to what you want the curriculum to achieve, particularly what the end goal is. What do we hope that our students will learn and remember? ... A builder does not begin the foundations before consulting the blueprints for how the house will look when it's finished. Teachers must do the same when building and writing their curriculum – start at the end.
>
> (pp60, 64)

Willingham (2009) emphasises that through the curriculum, teachers should aim to develop deep knowledge rather than shallow knowledge. This enables students not just to understand part of something but the whole of something. The curriculum helps students to connect previous pieces of shallow knowledge to make the knowledge deeper. Concepts need to be sequenced so that knowledge becomes deeper, resulting in schema modification. Concepts need to be continuously revisited, remembered and built on (Almond, 2020). Dylan Wiliam (2018) argues that, 'the purpose of the curriculum is to build up the content of long-term memory so that when students are asked to think, they are able to think in more powerful ways'. Learning should gradually increase in complexity as they move through the journey of the curriculum. If students are not learning more complex material as they progress through the curriculum, then the curriculum is not serving its purpose – helping students to know more, do more and remember more.

Coherence and sequencing are critically important. Rosenshine's second principle of instruction is to present new information to students in small steps. Teachers can think of the end goal and work backwards from this point. They can plan the steps that students need to take to achieve the end goal. These steps form the basis of individual lessons. It sounds easy, but it isn't – it requires hard thinking.

Lemov and Badillo (2020) believe that students should be comfortable with the idea of struggle. Learning is not easy, and it will require effort on the part of the student to accommodate new information into existing information, resulting in schema modification. We can make it easier for students by thinking carefully about how we sequence curriculum content and by chunking information into smaller components. Christine Counsell (2020) argues that there is a danger when curriculum quality is determined through proxies, including the proxy of assessment, because assessments rarely provide enough information about what pupils are learning. She argues that a grade 4 at GCSE represents a very low baseline and is not an indicator that students have deep knowledge of a subject. If a student has achieved a grade 4, there are aspects of the curriculum that are not secure or that they have not experienced. Arguably, even a student who achieves a grade 1 may not have deep knowledge. They may just have practised the material necessary to pass the exam, and the exam doesn't cover the full domain of a subject. Exam results are therefore not an indicator of curriculum quality. Counsell argues that the curriculum itself should be planned as a progression model. It is not sufficient to use grade or level descriptors as an indicator of curriculum progression because these do not identify everything that a student needs to know. They only identify the content which is being assessed. Finally, she argues that school leaders should not look for the application of cognitive science in lessons and use this as an indicator of curriculum quality. It does not mean that just because a teacher is using interleaving or retrieval practice that the curriculum is good. It is only good if students are deepening their knowledge.

iN THE CLASSROOM

History teachers might identify a subject-specific concept such as 'democracy'. They will then need to consider how to sequence students' understanding of this concept across Key Stage 3 and Key Stage 4. Within each year group, this concept might be revisited, and teachers might further develop students' understanding of the concept each time it is revisited. Consider how this might work within your subject. Identify a subject-specific concept and sequence the concept across the secondary phase so that students revisit the concept and deepen their understanding at each key revisiting point.

━━ TAKE 5 ━━

- All students are entitled to develop cultural capital.

- Providing students with cultural capital through the curriculum acts as a leveller by reducing the gap between advantaged and disadvantaged students.

- Accurate curriculum sequencing is important because it aids progression of knowledge, understanding and skills.

- Initial schemas are modified as students are introduced to increasingly complex subject content.

- The National Curriculum and examination syllabi are not carefully sequenced and do not necessarily identify the component knowledge that students need before they can master composite knowledge.

SUMMARY

This chapter has explored the concept of powerful knowledge. We have argued that the curriculum plays a critical role in providing students with cultural capital. Cultural capital enables students to access opportunities that might not be available to them if they did not have it. These include educational, social and cultural opportunities. Although we have not emphasised the role of the curriculum in promoting social justice and inclusion, this was a key point that we made in Chapter 1. School curricula should therefore be designed to address matters related to disability, sexuality, race, ethnicity and gender. These aspects are rarely addressed in curriculum policy documents and inspection frameworks but, nonetheless, the curriculum should seek to transform students' attitudes, values and beliefs about inclusion.

12
EDUCATION MYTHS

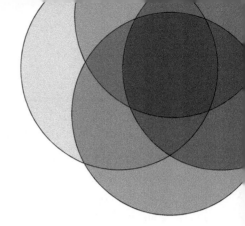

TEACHERS' STANDARDS

This chapter addresses elements of TS3, TS4, TS5, TS6 and TS8.

IN THIS CHAPTER

This chapter addresses some key educational myths. We outline the myths and explain why these are harmful. We focus on myths about intelligence, learning styles, grouping arrangements, experiential learning and motivation. It is important that teachers draw on evidence to support the pedagogical approaches that they choose to adapt. Over the last few decades, myths about what constitutes effective teaching have been internalised and accepted rather than being questioned. This has resulted in teachers adopting classroom practices that are not underpinned by robust evidence. We argue that an evidence-based approach is essential and that teachers should always ask for the evidence to substantiate pedagogical approaches when specific approaches are held up as being the gold standard.

KEY POLICY DOCUMENTATION

The *ITT Core Content Framework* states that trainees must learn that:

> There is a common misconception that pupils have distinct and identifiable learning styles. This is not supported by evidence and attempting to tailor lessons to learning styles is unlikely to be beneficial.

> (DfE, 2019a, p11)

This is one myth that is specifically identified in the CCF, but this chapter addresses a range of education myths.

DEBUNKING THE MYTHS

Education is a sector that is full of myths. Some of the myths are based on ideology rather than evidence of what works, and some arise from systemic practices that occur within schools. Clearly, research evidence can only take us so far. Just because research has demonstrated the efficacy of a particular pedagogical approach does not guarantee that the approach will work with every student, in every class and every school. Schools are complex organisations and student learning is also complex.

That said, research is important. Teaching is an academic vocation. Teachers, like doctors, need to master substantive, disciplinary and pedagogical knowledge before they practice. If they don't engage with educational research, there is a danger that they will adopt approaches in their own teaching that they observed their own teachers using when they were at school. This is not good enough.

The problem with education is that myths become practice. One example of this is the myth that teachers need to limit their time talking and that too much teacher talk reduces students' learning (Enser, 2019). This assumption is illogical. The teacher is the subject expert in the room. They have mastered the subject, they understand the subject-specific concepts and knowledge, and they are well-positioned to pass this information on to students. The problem is that people make assumptions that are not true. Just because a teacher is talking does not mean that students are passive learners. Effective teachers engage students effectively. They elicit responses from students through effective questioning to check their understanding and their teaching is responsive to the students' needs through carefully adapting it within the moment. They model and explain and then provide opportunities for guided practice before allowing students to work on the subject content independently. Teacher talk is therefore crucial to student learning.

This is one example of a myth. Another myth is that the last few minutes of a lesson should be devoted to a plenary to check students' understanding. Firstly, teachers should check students' understanding continuously throughout a lesson. Secondly, if teachers discover that students have misconceptions in the plenary, it is too late to do anything about it at that point (Enser, 2019).

We need to know the evidence that supports our pedagogical approaches. The Education Endowment Foundation and the Chartered College of Teaching have produced excellent research in recent years that can inform educational practice. As educators, we need to be willing to challenge myths such as the suggestion that future attainment can be reliably predicted based on past attainment, because it cannot. Unfortunately, this myth has resulted in the use of 'flight paths' in schools to predict students' progress and attainment, resulting in a lot of wasted time – time which could be better spent focusing on approaches that are more likely to have an impact. The following section identifies and debunks some of the key myths that teachers need to be aware of.

MYTH: RICH EXPERIENCES LEAD TO LEARNING

Through numerous examples, Claire Sealy (2019) has demonstrated that providing children with rich experiences does not always lead to learning gains. Sealy emphasises that information is stored in either the episodic memory or the semantic memory. The episodic memory is highly contextual. We store a quantity of superfluous information in this part of our memory that relates to experiences that we have had, but a great deal of this information does not relate to the things that we really need to remember. Students might remember participating in an educational visit. In their episodic memory, they will remember the experience of travelling to the place of interest, perhaps what they had for lunch and the things they did during the visit. However, they are not always able to communicate what they learned through these experiences. This might be because the episodic memory is limited and heavily anchored within contexts (Sealy, 2019), including sensory experiences. The semantic memory does not have the limitations of the episodic memory and is central to long-term learning (Sealy, 2019). For information to be stored in the semantic memory, teachers must provide students with opportunities to engage with the subject content, to work with it, to think hard about it, to retrieve it and to do something with it. Only then is it more likely to stick. When teachers do these things, they help students to form semantic memories.

Fun lessons that are crammed full of exciting activities can unintentionally prevent learning from happening (Sealy, 2019). The information goes into the episodic memory. Students can remember the activities they did rather than the critical things that teachers need them to learn. So much mental energy is spent on the practical elements of the lesson that students then do not have enough cognitive bandwidth to think hard about the concepts that they need to learn (Sealy, 2019). If students do not learn scientific concepts before they engage in practical science lessons, it is unlikely that they will learn those concepts through simply working scientifically. The experience will be committed to their episodic memory and not to their semantic memory. If students are required to spend time researching information themselves in subjects such as history, geography or religious education, the cognitive effort that they apply to the task of searching for relevant information results in less cognitive bandwidth for understanding subject-specific concepts and knowledge. Students need to know and understand the substantive knowledge of each subject before investing mental energy into student-led investigations, student-led problem-solving and collaborative learning. Concepts are likely to not become embedded unless they are revisited and retrieved.

MYTH: STUDENTS HAVE DIFFERENT LEARNING STYLES

It is important for students to know how to enhance their learning by drawing on a wide range of modalities (Coffield et al., 2004a, 2004b), essentially because students need to use different modalities to complete different kinds of tasks. Effective learners do not rely on one learning style. According to Coffield et al. (2004a, 2004b), there is no substantial evidence that matching learning style to tasks (matching hypothesis) increases educational attainment. In fact, evidence from empirical matching studies is contradictory (Coffield et al., 2004a, 2004b). It is therefore unwise to base pedagogical decisions upon inconclusive research evidence. Coffield et al. (2004a, 2004b) argue that learning styles can artificially restrict students' learning experience by limiting channels through which learning takes place. Learning style theory also leads to the assumption that learners have a fixed style of learning that is static (Coffield et al., 2004a, 2004b). This is an unwise assumption for both teachers and students because it limits the opportunities for learning.

MYTH: INTELLIGENCE IS FIXED

Research demonstrates that the brain can physically change and that this can occur well into adulthood (Abiola and Dhindsa, 2012). Research undertaken by Maguire et al. (2006) examined the physical changes in the brain in individuals undertaking training to become London taxi drivers. The research demonstrated that, following the training, there was a significant growth in the hippocampus, the area of the brain that processes spatial information (Maguire et al., 2006). Research that demonstrates the plasticity of the brain supports the belief that intellectual ability can be enhanced and developed through learning (Sternberg, 2005). It therefore supports the idea of a 'growth mindset' (Dweck, 1999). Individuals with growth mindsets believe that intelligence can grow and be developed through effort. In contrast, those with fixed mindsets view intelligence as a static trait and not something which can be developed.

Research demonstrates that two individuals with differing mindsets can start out at the same academic level, but over time the individual with the growth mindset will begin to outperform the individual with the fixed mindset (Dweck, 2009). Blackwell et al. (2007) found that throughout the duration of a two-year study, adolescent students with a fixed mindset did not show any improvement in their academic achievements. However, the achievements of the students that had been identified as having a growth mindset did show improvement. Research demonstrates that students who have a growth mindset achieve significantly better grades than their peers with a fixed mindset (Aronson et al., 2002; Blackwell et al., 2007). Research demonstrates that 'at every socioeconomic level, those who hold more of a growth mindset consistently outperform those who do not' (Claro et al., 2016, p8667). Fixed-ability thinking can encourage inequality (Boaler, 2013) because individuals with fixed mindsets may lack motivation and resilience and may not be prepared to invest effort into developing their brain. In the worst cases, these individuals give up on learning and develop 'learned helplessness'.

MYTH: MOTIVATION INCREASES LEARNING

Research demonstrates that improving achievement enhances motivation and confidence. It has been argued that:

Teachers who are confronted with the poor motivation and confidence of low attaining students may interpret this as the cause of their low attainment and assume that it is both necessary and possible to address their motivation before attempting to teach them new material. In fact, the evidence shows that attempts to enhance motivation in this way are unlikely to achieve that end. Even if they do, the impact on subsequent learning is close to zero ... the poor motivation of low attainers is a logical response to repeated failure. Start getting them to succeed and their motivation and confidence should increase.

(Coe et al., 2014, p23)

MYTH: iNTELLiGENCE iS PURELY GENETiC

A combination of both genetic factors and early experiences shape neuronal connections which develop neural circuits. These enable increasingly complex mental activities to occur (Moore, 2015; Slavich and Cole, 2013). As these circuits become increasingly stable, they contribute to the development of complex thoughts, skills and behaviours in individuals (Cantor et al., 2019). Environmental and interpersonal experiences influence brain growth throughout childhood and well into adulthood. It has been demonstrated that 'genes act as followers, not prime movers, in developmental processes' (Cantor et al., 2019, p309). It has also been demonstrated that positive, nurturing relationships are essential to brain development. These relationships build strong brain architecture (Cantor et al., 2019). We know that children's development is shaped by micro-ecological contexts (i.e. families, peers, schools and communities) as well as macro-ecological contexts (i.e. economic and cultural systems).

The brain is characterised by plasticity rather than stability. Its structure is influenced not just by genetics but by the micro and macro contexts within which individuals are situated. Physical, psychological, social and emotional processes also influence brain structure. Emotions can have powerful effects on developmental pathways (Cantor et al., 2019). The implications of this are significant because the research demonstrates that an individual's experiences can shape the development of neural pathways which facilitate mental processes. Thus, exposure to high-quality teaching can change the structure of the brain by activating new neural pathways.

The evidence from research has demonstrated that:

- children's learning and development is shaped by a combination of environmental factors and learning opportunities both inside and outside schools;

- learning involves physical, psychological, social and emotional processes. These influence one another in that the interactions between these processes can enable or restrict learning;

- the brain and intelligence are malleable and can be changed by environmental influences, including exposure to high-quality teaching;

- our experiences activate neural pathways that enable new ways of thinking and new skills to develop;

- emotions and social contexts shape neural connections which contribute to attention, concentration and memory as well as knowledge transfer and application. Research has demonstrated that chronic stress due to trauma affects cognition and working memory;

- differentiated instruction enables optimum brain growth.

(Darling-Hammond et al., 2020)

MYTH: ABiLiTY GROUPiNG iMPROVES ATTAiNMENT

The research on grouping arrangements has been largely inconclusive. Some studies indicate positive effects on attainment and others suggest null effects (Slavin, 1987) or detrimental effects on the attainment of students who are assigned to lower ability groups (Slavin, 1990). The problem with ability groups is that they can encourage a fixed mindset in both students and teachers. If teachers start to believe that some students are not very able, this can result in reduced expectations of them and assigning tasks which do not push them to the limits of their potential. In addition, ability grouping can place a ceiling on students' achievements because they may not be exposed to more challenging subject content. Additionally, students in lower ability groups can start to develop learned helplessness (Butkowsky and Willows, 1980) and they can disengage from learning and develop poor self-esteem (Felmlee and Eder, 1983).

Hart et al. (2004) have demonstrated the negative effects of grouping students by attainment. These include reduced teachers' expectations, undermining students' dignity and sense of hope, and access to a restricted curriculum for students in low attainment groups. Slavin's research (1987, 1990) has demonstrated that ability grouping did not increase average student achievement but impacted detrimentally on the achievement of students in lower ability groups. Advocates of ability grouping emphasise the associated benefits of differentiated teaching and the importance of tailoring the curriculum and pedagogy to the needs of individual students (Tomlinson, 2000). However, research highlights the dangers of grouping and teaching students on the basis of achievement data, particularly for students in lower attainment groups (Francis et al., 2017).

According to Coe et al. (2014):

> Although ability grouping can in theory allow teachers to target a narrower range of pace and content of lessons, it can also create an exaggerated sense of within-group homogeneity and between-group heterogeneity in the teacher's mind (Stipek, 2010).

(p23)

MYTH: DIFFERENTIATION IS GOOD

According to Ashman (2019b):

> *Differentiation as we know it is overhyped. There is very little evidence that practices that are commonly classified as aspects of differentiation make any significant difference to the quality of teaching – and there are, in some instances, good reasons to suspect that they may have a negative effect.*

(p49)

Examples of such strategies include placing learners into sets or ability groups, matching tasks to students' supposed learning styles and setting completely different activities for specific groups of students or individuals. Terwel (2005) argues that differentiation has led to the emergence of inequality in classrooms because it widens the ability gap. It has been suggested that the practice of differentiation in classrooms has been largely unsuccessful (Hertberg-Davis, 2009) and restricted opportunities for learning for specific students (Taylor, 2017). Although differentiation has been promoted as a pedagogical approach for at least three decades, the *Education Inspection Framework* (Ofsted, 2019) states that teachers should 'adapt their teaching as necessary, without unnecessarily elaborate or differentiated approaches' (p9).

MYTH: DIRECT INSTRUCTION IS INEFFECTIVE

Recent evidence suggests that direct instruction rather than 'discovery learning' is highly effective in promoting learning gains. According to Coe et al. (2014):

> *Enthusiasm for 'discovery learning' is not supported by research evidence, which broadly favours direct instruction (Kirschner et al., 2006). Although learners do need to build new understanding on what they already know, if teachers want them to learn new ideas, knowledge or methods they need to teach them directly.*

(p23)

Evidence supports the use of direct instructional guidance to students (Kirschner et al., 2006) rather than constructivist approaches that use minimal teacher guidance, particularly for novice and intermediate learners. Sherrington (2019a) differentiates between the use of constructivist approaches which influence what students are doing in the lesson (for example, collaborative group work) and constructivist thinking which students do individually. He argues that students need to make connections between new and existing knowledge and modify existing schemas (constructivist thinking), but he also emphasises that teacher-led instruction is essential in supporting students to construct knowledge. He argues that small group work and problem-solving approaches may play a role in consolidating prior learning but not as vehicles for making discoveries.

According to Ashman (2019b), the principles of direct teaching contradict those of enquiry-based learning models. In contrast, enquiry models focus on students discovering knowledge or working things out for themselves. However, evidence suggests that enquiry-based learning approaches are less effective than direct teaching (Kirschner et al., 2006). One of the reasons for this is that breaking information into bite-sized chunks and teaching it directly actually reduces cognitive load. In contrast, enquiry-based approaches risk overwhelming students with large amounts of information. This can overload the working memory (Ashman, 2019b) and result in students being exposed to large amounts of extraneous information.

KEY RESEARCH: SPOTLIGHTING THE KEY MYTHS

- The evidence suggests that providing students with generic praise (rather than specific praise) and praise which is not deserved when marking a piece of work is not beneficial. Praise may have negative consequences on students' self-evaluations of their ability, particularly if praise suggests to students that teachers have low expectations of what they can achieve (Hattie and Timperley, 2007).

- Enthusiasm for 'discovery learning' is not supported by research evidence, which broadly favours direct instruction (Kirschner et al., 2006).

- Evidence on the effects of grouping by ability suggests that it makes very little difference to learning outcomes (Higgins et al., 2014).

- The key to increasing student motivation is to get learners to increase their attainment through supporting them to succeed. There is no evidence that increasing motivation improves students' learning (Coe et al., 2014).

- There are no benefits for learning from trying to present information to learners in their preferred learning style (Geake, 2008; Howard-Jones, 2014; Pashler et al., 2009; Riener and Willingham, 2010).

- A range of studies have shown that self-testing, trying to generate answers and deliberately creating intervals between study to allow forgetting are all more effective approaches.

(Coe et al., 2014)

MYTH: INTELLIGENCE IS MORE IMPORTANT THAN GRIT

Research on 'grit' (Duckworth, 2017; Duckworth et al., 2007) suggests that this is an important characteristic which influences achievement. The term is sometimes used interchangeably with resilience. However, there are some key differences between grit and resilience. Resilience is usually used to describe overcoming situations of adversity, although this is not uncontroversial (for example, see Roffey, 2017). In contrast, grit is associated with sustained perseverance (Duckworth et al., 2007) towards long-term goals. Research demonstrates that grit is essential to high achievement, and seminal research has found that grit is more predictive of high achievement than IQ (Terman and Oden, 1947). Individuals with grit are able to stay focused on achieving long-term goals, even in the absence of instant gratification. They demonstrate a very high level of ability to stay focused on achieving their goals and are motivated by the accomplishment of the task that they are undertaking rather than extrinsic rewards.

MYTH: CURRiCULUM DESiGN DOES NOT AFFECT LEARNiNG

What is taught, how it is taught (Biesta, 2009) and who is included in the curriculum (Young, 2013) are key principles that underpin effective curriculum design. Research suggests that the humanities subjects have been marginalised from the primary curriculum (Barnes and Scoffham, 2017; Ofsted, 2002). In addition, research indicates that learners in receipt of pupil premium are less likely to take English Baccalaureate (EBacc) subjects compared with those not in receipt of pupil premium (Allen and Thompson, 2016).

International research demonstrates that curriculum narrowing is not specific to the United Kingdom. According to Berliner (2011), it has become commonplace across the United States in response to the pressures of high-stakes testing. In Australia, evidence suggests that testing regimes have led to a reduction in the time spent on non-assessed subjects and impacted detrimentally on classroom pedagogy (Polesel et al., 2014) as a result of teaching to the test. Research suggests that teachers have been discouraged from experimenting with teaching strategies in the quest to improve test results (Ofsted, 2019).

Effective sequencing of the curriculum and use of retrieval practice helps learners to remember content. Research also suggests that repeating and reviewing key concepts (Scheerens and Bosker, 1997; Seidel and Shavelson, 2007) by spacing out learning (distributed practice) is a key characteristic of effective curriculum planning. As Sweller et al. (2011) have pointed out, 'if nothing in the long-term memory has been altered, nothing has been learned'. An effective approach to curriculum planning is to block learning and repeat practice over time, with spaces in between revisiting content, as this leads to better long-term retention of knowledge (Rawson and Kintsch, 2005). There is also increasing evidence that interleaving can improve long-term retention (Richland et al., 2005; Rohrer et al., 2015). Interleaving is the sequencing of learning tasks so that similar but slightly different content or tasks are interspersed. This results in a more variable and challenging learning experience but leads to better long-term retention. Retrieval practice strengthens memory and aids long-term retention (Barenberg et al., 2018; Roediger and Karpicke, 2006).

MYTH: TESTiNG iS BAD

The assumption that testing and quizzing are detrimental to learners is a myth, as evidence suggests that the frequent use of low-stakes testing can contribute to learning in valuable ways. Research has demonstrated the importance of retrieval practice (Barenberg et al., 2018). This research shows strong evidence for the *testing effect*. This means that when students take a test shortly after studying a piece of material, they perform better on a final test than those who do not, even if no feedback is given on the initial test. This is because the process of testing knowledge forces retrieval. This evidence supports the use of frequent low-stakes testing within and between units of work. Davies (2020) suggests that formative assessment, such as multiple-choice quizzes, should be continuous and non-graded.

MYTH: TEACHiNG ASSiSTANTS ENHANCE STUDENT LEARNiNG

Research demonstrates that teaching assistants (TAs) spend most of their time supporting students with the highest level of need (Sharples et al., 2015). This limits opportunities for peer interaction and limits exposure to high-quality teaching by the teacher. Research demonstrates that the quality of instruction that students receive from teaching assistants is inferior to that provided by the teacher (Radford et al., 2011; Rubie-Davies et al., 2010). For example, evidence suggests that teaching assistants tend to close talk down and 'spoon-feed' answers (Radford et al., 2011; Rubie-Davies et al., 2010). Over time, this can limit understanding, weaken pupils' sense of control over their learning and reduce their capacity to develop independent learning skills (Sharples et al., 2015). According to Sharples et al. (2015, p12):

> *Those pupils receiving the most support from TAs made less progress than similar pupils who received little or no support from TAs. There was also evidence that the negative impact was most marked for pupils with the highest levels of SEN, who, as discussed, typically receive the most TA support.*

Evidence suggests that some deployment arrangements can foster student dependency rather than promoting independent learning, largely because they prioritise task completion rather than encouraging pupils to think for themselves (Moyles and Suschitzky, 1997). In addition, the over-reliance on one-to-one teaching-assistant support can lead to lack of ownership and responsibility for learning, and separation from peers (Giangreco, 2010). Research demonstrates that the average impact of teaching assistants delivering structured interventions is less than that for interventions using experienced qualified teachers (Sharples et al., 2015).

Research also suggests that although teaching assistants can have positive effects in relation to reducing teacher workload and reducing classroom disruption (Blatchford et al., 2012), levels of qualifications vary between teaching assistants, and opportunities for communication between teaching assistants and teachers can be minimal (Blatchford et al., 2012). This means that teaching assistants can be underprepared when they go into classrooms. The impact of TAs on student learning can be increased by ensuring that they can access high-quality professional development and training in the structured programmes that they are delivering (Sharples et al., 2015). Deploying TAs in this way has a greater impact on student outcomes than deployment arrangements which result in them providing general and unstructured support in classrooms (Sharples et al., 2015).

MYTH: TOO MUCH TEACHER TALK IS BAD

Key research findings are summarised below.

- Moreno (2004) concluded that there is a growing body of research showing that students learn more deeply from strongly guided learning.

- The worked-example effect, which has been replicated a number of times, provides some of the strongest evidence for the superiority of direct teaching. Thus, students learn more when given worked examples of problems because this reduces the load on the working memory (Kirschner et al., 2006).

- Direct guidance is necessary for both effective learning and transfer (Roblyer, 1996).

- Research consistently supports direct, strong instructional guidance rather than constructivist-based minimal guidance during teaching (Kirschner et al., 2006).

- Process worksheets have been found to be effective in promoting learning (Nadolski et al., 2005). These are worksheets which include worked examples, steps through problems, hints and tips.

The research demonstrates that students learn more through direct teacher guidance and this approach requires teachers to use dialogue in lessons.

MYTH: CLASSROOM DISPLAYS ENHANCE LEARNING

The ability to focus and sustain attention to important information is essential for learning in the classroom and it is positively associated with academic achievement (Erickson et al., 2015; McKinney et al., 1975; Oakes et al., 2002). Attention is the gateway to learning (Steele et al., 2012) and the more focused children are on a task, the better the learning outcome. As children get older, they sustain greater attention and even manage to stay focused when there are distractions (Gaspelin et al., 2015; Matusz et al., 2015), although their ability to focus varies between children of the same age.

Fisher et al. (2014) provided the first systematic exploration of the impact of visual displays on behaviour and learning in young children (mean age 5.5 years). They systematically manipulated the amount of visual information that children were exposed to in a lab classroom over six science lessons. Half of the lessons were delivered in a visually stimulating classroom and half were taught with no visual displays. Children visited the classroom for the six lessons over a two-week period and completed an assessment task at the end of each lesson. They were video recorded during the lessons and their behaviour was coded in relation to their visual engagement as either being on-task (e.g. looking at the teacher, looking at their books) or off-task (e.g. looking at peers, looking at the walls). In the classroom where displays were removed, children did engage in off-task behaviour. However, in the presence of lots of visual displays, children spent more time overall engaging in off-task behaviour compared to their behaviour in the classroom with no visual stimuli. Importantly, children performed significantly worse in terms of their learning in the highly visual classroom compared to their performance when in the classroom with no displays. More time spent off-task was related to poorer learning.

Emerging evidence therefore highlights that visual features of school classrooms, specifically wall displays, have implications for attention and learning (Barrett et al., 2015; Fisher et al., 2014). These studies provide the first empirical evidence for the possible detrimental impact of the visual classroom on learning.

iN THE CLASSROOM

Explicit and direct instruction is a robust teaching strategy and is supported by extensive research evidence. Explicit modelling of subject content and guided practice followed by independent work are strategies which are likely to lead to large learning gains. The teacher is the most important resource in the classroom. A significant proportion of lesson time should be devoted to explicit and direct instruction rather than discovery approaches to learning, which are less effective and increase cognitive load.

TAKE 5

- Intelligence is not fixed.
- There is no evidence that teaching students according to a pre-determined learning style has a positive effect and it is likely to be harmful.
- Explicit direct instruction is effective.
- Teacher talk is good, not bad.
- The frequent use of low-stakes testing promotes learning.

SUMMARY

Teachers should always maintain a sense of healthy scepticism when specific pedagogical approaches are promoted. Teachers should always be keen to read the research evidence which underpins specific approaches to determine whether they are likely to work in the classroom. That said, it is important to remember that research also needs to be critically evaluated. Students' learning is significantly influenced by specific contexts, including those of school, teachers, family and community. Evidence-based approaches might be determined to be successful in one context, but these approaches might be ineffective in another context. Students also vary and specific approaches which work with one student might not work with another student. The Chartered College for Teaching and the Education Endowment Foundation provide some excellent summaries of large-scale research projects. Teachers should critically evaluate these research studies, considering the contexts of their own school, students and classrooms.

CONCLUSION

This book has provided a useful synthesis of key research in relation to specific pedagogical approaches in education. We have argued in various chapters that students benefit from explicit direct instruction. We have emphasised the need to introduce subject content in small chunks, with regular ongoing teacher assessment and guided and independent practice after each step. We have stressed the need for a well-sequenced curriculum so that students can connect new learning to prior learning, and we introduced key substantive content on memory to support your understanding of cognitive load. Practical retrieval strategies have been outlined and we have included strategies for reducing cognitive load.

We have acknowledged Black and Wiliam's (1998, 2005) contribution to assessment. We have argued that regular testing of knowledge is vital in facilitating retrieval and we have made a case for the use of low-stakes multiple-choice assessments to provide both teachers and students with information in relation to how much knowledge has been retained. We have argued that the curriculum needs to be viewed as a progression model that outlines all the essential knowledge that students need to acquire and the steps that they need to take to develop fluent knowledge. We have highlighted the fact that examinations do not assess the breadth of knowledge that students need to acquire. There is a need to shift our thinking away from examinations as a form of assessment if schools are to develop approaches to assessment that systematically check that students have acquired fluent knowledge across the full breadth of a subject domain.

We have argued in favour of a knowledge-rich curriculum. Access to knowledge is a leveller. It reduces inequality and improves life outcomes. Students who are disadvantaged may not have access to the cultural and linguistic capitals that more advantaged students have access to. Schools therefore have a duty to provide all students with powerful knowledge – the best of what has been said and thought – so that all students can access networks, opportunities and organisations where knowledge is a pre-requisite for gaining entry. More significantly, knowledge enables students to contribute to and lead debates and it enriches lives. Teaching students to the test results in the dilution of substantive subject content, and high-stakes examinations only scratch the surface of what students need to know, understand and be able to do. We have argued that knowledge, curriculum design and assessment are therefore inextricably linked.

Conclusion

We have debunked several educational myths and presented a case for explicit, direct and responsive teaching. However, we wish to finish by emphasising that we do not want readers to think that we are promoting didactic approaches. In explicit and direct teaching, the teacher must ensure that they are responding to student misconceptions, checking student understanding of each step and developing strategies to actively engage all students in the process of thinking.

REFERENCES

Abiola, O.O. and Dhindsa, H.S. (2012) 'Improving classroom practices using our knowledge of how the brain works', *International Journal of Environmental and Science Education*, 7(1): 71–81.

Alexander, R.J. (2017) *Towards Dialogic Teaching: Rethinking Classroom Talk* (5th edn), Thirsk: Dialogos.

Allen, R. and Thomson, D. (2016) 'Changing the subject: how are the EBacc and Attainment 8 reforms changing results?', London: The Sutton Trust.

Almond, N. (2020) 'Curriculum coherence: how best to do it?', in C. Sealy and T. Bennett (eds), *The ResearchED Guide to the Curriculum: An Evidence-Informed Guide for Teachers*, Melton, UK: John Catt Educational, pp59–70.

Aronson, J., Fried, C. and Good, C. (2002) 'Reducing the effects of stereotype threat on African American college students by shaping theories of intelligence', *Journal of Experimental Social Psychology*, 38: 113–25.

Ashbee, R. (2020) 'Why is it so important to understand school subjects – and how we might begin to do so', in C. Sealy and T. Bennett (eds), *The ResearchED Guide to the Curriculum: An Evidence-Informed Guide for Teachers*, Melton, UK: John Catt Educational, pp31–40.

Ashman, G. (2019a) 'The differentiation myth', in C. Barton and T. Bennett (eds), *The ResearchED Guide to Education Myths: An Evidence-Informed Guide for Teachers*, Melton, UK: John Catt Educational, pp49–56.

Ashman, G. (2019b) 'Explicit teaching', in A. Boxer and T. Bennett (eds), *The ResearchED Guide to Explicit and Direct Instruction*, Melton, UK: John Catt Educational, pp29–35.

Baddeley, A.D. (2000) 'The episodic buffer: a new component of working memory?', *Trends in Cognitive Sciences*, 4(11): 417–23.

Baddeley, A.D. and Hitch, G.J. (1974) 'Working memory', in G.A. Bower (ed.), *The Psychology of Learning and Motivation: Advances in Research and Theory*, New York: Academic Press, 47–89.

Bandura, A. (1977) *Social Learning Theory*, New York: General Learning Press.

Barenberg, J. and Dutke, S. (2019) 'Testing and metacognition: retrieval practise effects on metacognitive monitoring in learning from text', *Memory*, 27(3): 269–79, available at: doi: 10.1080/09658211.2018.1506481

Barenberg, J., Roeder, U.R. and Dutke, S. (2018) 'Students' temporal distributing of learning activities in psychology courses: factors of influence and effects on the metacognitive learning outcome', *Psychology Learning and Teaching*, 17(3): 257–71.

Barnes, J. and Scoffham, S. (2017) 'The humanities in English primary schools: struggling to survive', *Education*, 45(3): 3–13.

Barrett, P., Davies, F., Zhang, Y. and Barrett, L. (2015) 'The impact of classroom design on pupils' learning: final results of a holistic, multilevel analysis', *Building and Environment*, 89: 118–33.

Bembenutty, H. and Karabenick, S. (2004) 'Inherent association between academic delay of gratification, future time perspective, and self-regulated learning', *Educational Psychology Review*, 16(1): 35–57.

Berliner, D. (2011) 'Rational responses to high stakes testing: the case of curriculum narrowing and the harm that follows', *Cambridge Journal of Education*, 41(3): 287–302.

Biesta, G. (2009) 'Good education in an age of measurement: on the need to reconnect with the question of purpose in education', *Educational Assessment, Evaluation and Accountability*, 21(1): 33–46.

Bjork, E.L. and Bjork, R.A. (2011) 'Making things hard on yourself, but in a good way: creating desirable difficulties to enhance learning', in M.A. Gernsbacher, R.W. Pew, L.M. Hough and J.R. Pomerantz (eds), *Psychology and the Real World: Essays Illustrating Fundamental Contributions to Society*, New York: Worth Publishers, pp56–64.

Black, P. and Wiliam, D. (1998) *Inside the Black Box: Raising Standards Through Classroom Assessment*, Phi Delta Kappan.

Black, P. and Wiliam, D. (2005) *Inside the Black Box: Raising Standards Through Classroom Assessment*, London: Granada Learning.

Blackwell, L.S., Trzesniewski, K.H. and Dweck, C.S. (2007) 'Implicit theories of intelligence predict achievement across an adolescent transition: a longitudinal study and an intervention', *Child Development*, 78(1): 246–63.

Blake, J. (2019) 'All children can be taught: the relationship between pedagogy, curriculum and explicit instruction, and why this supports pupils with low prior attainment', in A. Boxer and T. Bennett (eds), *The ResearchED Guide to Explicit and Direct Instruction*, Melton, UK: John Catt Educational, pp139–46.

Blankson, A.N., Weaver, J.M., Leerkes, E.M., O'Brien, M., Calkins, S.D. and Marcovitch, S. (2016) 'Cognitive and emotional processes as predictors of a successful transition into school', *Early Education and Development*, 28(1): 1–20.

Blatchford, P., Russell, A. and Webster, R. (2012) *Reassessing the Impact of Teaching Assistants: How Research Challenges Practice and Policy*, Abingdon, UK: Routledge.

Bligh, C. (2014) *The Silent Experiences of Young Bilingual Learners*, Rotterdam: Sense Publishers.

Boaler, J. (2013) 'Ability and mathematics: the mindset revolution that is reshaping education', *Forum*, 55(1): 143–52.

Boekaerts, M. (1999) 'Motivated learning: studying student * situation transactional units', *European Journal of Psychology of Education*, 14(1): 41–55, available at: https://doi.org/10.1007/BF03173110

Bouffard, T., Marcoux, M., Vezeau, C. and Bordeleau, L. (2003) 'Changes in self-perceptions of competence and intrinsic motivation among elementary school children', *British Journal of Educational Psychology*, 73(2): 171–86.

Bourdieu, P. (1984) *Distinction: A Social Critique of the Judgement of Taste*, Cambridge, MA: Harvard University Press.

Braaksma, M.A.H., Rijlaarsdam, G. and van den Bergh, H. (2002) 'Observational learning and the effects of model-observer similarity', *Journal of Educational Psychology*, 94(2): 405–15.

Bradlow, J., Bartram, F., Guasp, A. and Jadva, V. (2017) 'School report: the experiences of lesbian, gay, bi and trans young people in Britain's schools in 2017', London: Stonewall, available at: http://www.stonewall.org.uk/school-report-2017

Brookhart, S.M. (2001) 'Successful students' formative and summative uses of assessment information', *Assessment in Education*, 8(2): 153–69.

Bruner, J.S. (1978) 'The role of dialogue in language acquisition', in A. Sinclair, R.J. Jarvelle and W.J.M. Levelt (eds), *The Student's Concept of Language*, New York: Springer-Verlag, 241–256.

Butkowsky, I.S. and Willows, D.M. (1980) 'Cognitive-motivational characteristics of children varying in reading ability: evidence for learned helplessness in poor readers', *Journal of Educational Psychology*, 72(3): 408–22.

Butler, R. (1987) 'Task-involving and ego-involving properties of evaluation: effects of different feedback conditions on motivational perceptions, interest, and performance', *Journal of Educational Psychology*, 79(4): 474–82.

Cambridge Assessment (2019) 'Metacognition', available at: www.cambridgeinternational. org/Images/272307-metacognition.pdf

Cantor, P., Osher, D., Berg, J., Steyer, L. and Rose, T. (2019) 'Malleability, plasticity, and individuality: how children learn and develop in context', *Applied Developmental Science*, 23(4): 307–37.

Carvalho, P.F. and Goldstone, R.L. (2014) 'Effects of interleaved and blocked study on delayed test of category learning generalization', *Frontiers in Psychology*, 5, available at: https://www.frontiersin.org/article/10.3389/fpsyg.2014.00936

Chandler, P. and Sweller, J. (1991) 'Cognitive load theory and the format of instruction', *Cognition and Instruction*, 8(4): 293–332.

Christodoulou, D. (2017) *Making Good Progress? The Future of Assessment for Learning*, Oxford: Open University Press.

Claro, S., Pauneskub, D. and Dweck, C.S. (2016) 'Growth mindset tempers the effects of poverty on academic achievement', *PNAS*, available at: https://web.stanford.edu/~paunesku/articles/claro_2016.pdf

Coe, R., Aloisi, C., Higgins, S. and Major, L.E. (2014) *What Makes Great Teaching? Review of the Underpinning Research, Project Report*, London: Sutton Trust.

Coffield, F., Moseley, D., Hall, E. and Ecclestone, K. (2004a) *Should We Be Using Learning Styles? What Research Has to Say to Practice*, London: Learning and Skills Research Centre, Learning and Skills Development Agency.

Coffield, F., Moseley, D., Hall, E. and Ecclestone, K. (2004b) *Learning Styles and Pedagogy in Post-16 Learning: A Systematic and Critical Review*, London: Learning and Skills Research Centre, Learning and Skills Development Agency.

Condie, R., Livingston, K. and Seagraves, L. (2005) *Evaluation of the Assessment for Learning Programme: Final Report*, Glasgow: Quality in Education Centre, University of Strathclyde.

Coombe, A. and Martin, L. (2019) 'Using direct instruction to teach writing: secondary English', in A. Boxer and T. Bennett (eds), *The ResearchED Guide to Explicit and Direct Instruction*, Melton, UK: John Catt Educational, pp95–107.

Counsell, C. (2018) 'Taking the curriculum seriously', *Impact*, 4, available at: https://impact.chartered.college/article/taking-curriculum-seriously/

Counsell, C. (2020) 'Better conversations with subject leaders', in C. Sealy and T. Bennett (eds), *The ResearchED Guide to the Curriculum: An Evidence-Informed Guide for Teachers*, Melton, UK: John Catt Educational, pp95–121.

Creemers, B.P.M. and Kyriakides, L. (2006) 'Critical analysis of the current approaches to modelling educational effectiveness: The importance of establishing a dynamic model', *School Effectiveness and School Improvement*, 17: 347–66, available at: http://www.rug.nl/staff/b.p.m.creemers/testing_the_dynamic_model_of_educational_effectiveness.pdf

Creemers, B.P.M. and Kyriakides, L. (2011) *Improving Quality in Education: Dynamic Approaches to School Improvement*, Abingdon, UK: Routledge.

Cullen, S. (2019) 'Fading: removing teacher presence in directed teaching', in A. Boxer and T. Bennett (eds), *The ResearchED Guide to Explicit and Direct Instruction*, Melton, UK: John Catt Educational, pp87–94.

Cummins, J. (1980) 'Psychological assessment of immigrant children: logic or intuition?' *Journal of Multilingual and Multicultural Development*, 1(2): 97–111.

Daniel, G., Wang, C. and Berthelsen, D. (2016) 'Early school-based parent involvement, children's self-regulated learning and academic achievement: an Australian longitudinal study', *Early Childhood Research Quarterly*, 36(2): 168–77.

Darling-Hammond, L., Flook, L., Cook-Harvey, C., Barron, B. and Osher, D. (2020) 'Implications for educational practice of the science of learning and development', *Applied Developmental Science*, 24(2): 97–140.

Davies, J., Hallam, S. and Ireson, J. (2003) 'Ability groupings in the primary school: issues arising from practice', *Research Papers in Education*, 18(1): 45–60.

Davies, R. (2020) 'Strength in numbers: operationalising a network-wide assessment model', in S. Donarski and T. Bennett (eds), *The ResearchED Guide to Assessment: An Evidence-Informed Guide for Teachers*, Melton, UK: John Catt Educational, pp73–90.

Davis, P. and Florian, F. (2004) *Teaching Strategies and Approaches for Pupils with Special Educational Needs: A Scoping Study Research Report (RR516)*, London: DfES.

De Bruyckere, P. (2018) *The Ingredients for Great Teaching*, London: Sage.

Department for Education (DfE) (2011) *Teachers' Standards Guidance for School Leaders, School Staff and Governing Bodies*, London: DfE.

Department for Education (DfE) (2019a) *ITT Core Content Framework*, London: DfE.

Department for Education (DfE) (2019b) *Early Career Framework*, London: DfE.

Department for Education (DfE) and Department of Health (DoH) (2015) *Special Educational Needs and Disability Code of Practice*, London: DfE & DoH.

Dinsmore, D., Alexander, P. and Loughlin, S. (2008) 'Focusing the conceptual lens on meta-cognition, self-regulation, and self-regulated learning', *Educational Psychology Review*, 20(4): 391–409.

Dixon, A. (2002) 'Editorial', *Forum*, 44(1): 1.

Duckworth, A. (2017) *Grit: The Power of Passion and Perseverance*, New York: Vermilion.

Duckworth, A.L., Peterson, C., Matthews, M.D. and Kelly, D.R. (2007) 'Grit: perseverance and passion for long-term goals', *Journal of Personality and Social Psychology*, 92(6): 1087–101.

Dunlosky, J., Rawson, K.A., Marsh, E.J., Nathan, M.J. and Willingham, D.T. (2013) 'Improving students' learning with effective learning techniques: promising directions from cognitive and educational psychology', *Psychological Science in the Public Interest*, 14(1): 4–58, available at: doi: 10.1177/1529100612453266

Dweck, C.S. (1999) *Self-Theories: Their Role in Motivation, Personality, and Development*, Hove: Psychology Press.

Dweck, C.S. (2007) 'Boosting achievement with messages that motivate', *Education Canada*, 47(2): 6–10.

Dweck, C.S. (2009) 'Mindsets: developing talent through a growth mindset', *Olympic Coach*, 21(1): 4–7.

Dweck, C.S. (2010) 'Giving students meaningful work', *Educational Leadership*, 68(1): 16–20.

Ebbinghaus, H. (1885) *Über das Gedächtnis*, Leipzig: Dunker.

Education Endowment Foundation (EEF) (2018) *Metacognition and Self-Regulated Learning*, London: EEF.

Education Endowment Foundation (2021) *Cognitive Science Approaches in the Classroom: A Review of the Evidence*, London: EEF.

Engelmann, S. (1993) 'The curriculum as the cause of failure', *Oregon Conference Monograph Journal*, 5(2): 3–8.

Engelmann, S. and Carnine, D. (1982) *Theory of Instruction: Principles and Applications*, New York: Irvington Press.

Enser, M. (2019) 'Education myths: an origin story', in C. Barton and T. Bennett (eds), *The ResearchED guide to Education Myths: An Evidence-Informed Guide for Teachers*, Melton, UK: John Catt Educational, pp19–28.

Erickson, L.C., Thiessen, E.D., Godwin, K.E., Dickerson, J.P. and Fisher, A.V. (2015) 'Endogenously and exogenously driven selective sustained attention: contributions to learning in kindergarten children', *Journal of Experimental Child Psychology*, 138: 126–34.

Farrington, C.A., Roderick, M., Allensworth, E., Nagaoka, J., Keyes, T.S., Johnson, D.W. and Beechum, N.O. (2012) *Teaching Adolescents to Become Learners: The Role of Noncognitive Factors in Shaping School Performance – A Critical Literature Review*, Chicago, IL: University of Chicago Consortium on Chicago School Research.

Felmlee, D. and Eder, D. (1983) 'Contextual effects in the classroom: the impact of ability groups on student attainment', *Sociology of Education*, 56: 77–87.

Fisher, A.V., Godwin, K.E. and Seltman, H. (2014) 'Visual environment, attention allocation, and learning in young children: when too much of a good thing may be bad', *Psychological Science*, 25: 1362–70.

Flórez, M.T. and Sammons, P. (2013) *Assessment for Learning: Effects and Impact*, Berkshire: CfBT Education Trust.

Francis, B., Archer, L., Hodgen, J., Pepper, D., Taylor, B. and Travers, M. (2017) 'Exploring the relative lack of impact of research on "ability grouping" in England: a discourse-analytic account', *Cambridge Journal of Education*, 47(1): 1–17.

Furst, E. (2018) 'From neuroscience to the classroom', *ResearchED*, 2: 32–5, available at: https://researched.org.uk/wp-content/uploads/2020/03/researchEDMagazine-Sept2018-web-1.pdf

Garon-Carrier, G., Boivin, M., Guay, F., Kovas, Y., Dionne, G., Lemelin, J., Seguin, J.R., Vitaro, F. and Tremblay, R.E. (2016) 'Intrinsic motivation and achievement in mathematics in elementary schools: a longitudinal investigation of their association', *Child Development*, 87(1): 166–7.

Gaspelin, N., Margett-Jordan, T. and Ruthruff, E. (2015) 'Susceptible to distraction: children lack top-down control over spatial attention capture', *Psychonomic Bulletin & Review*, 22: 461–8.

Geake, J. (2008) 'Neuromythologies in education', *Educational Research*, 50(2): 123–33.

Georghiades, P. (2004) 'From the general to the situated: three decades of metacognition', *International Journal of Science Education*, 26(3): 365–83.

Giangreco, M.F. (2010) 'One-to-one paraprofessionals for students with disabilities in inclusive classrooms: is conventional wisdom wrong?' *Intellectual & Developmental Disabilities*, 48(1): 1–13.

Gipps, C., McCallum, B., Hargreaves, E. and Pickering, A. (2005) 'From TA to assessment for learning: the impact of assessment policy on teachers' assessment practice', Paper presented at the *British Educational Research Association Annual Conference*, University of Glamorgan, 14–17 September 2005.

Goldstein, E.B. (2011) *Cognitive Psychology: Mind, Research and Everyday Experience* (3rd edn), Belmont, CA: Wadsworth Cengage Learning.

Gorard, S. (2010) 'Education can compensate for society – a bit', *British Journal of Educational Studies*, 58(1): 47–65, available at: https://doi.org/10.1080/00071000903516411

Graham S. and Harris, K.R. (1994) 'The role and development of self-regulation in the writing process', in D.H. Schunk and B.J. Zimmerman (eds), *Self-Regulation of Learning and Performance: Issues and Educational Applications*, Hillsdale, NJ: Lawrence Erlbaum, pp203–28.

Hart, S., Dixon, A., Drummond, M.J. and McIntyre, D. (2004) *Learning without Limits*, Maidenhead, UK: Open University Press.

Harter, S. (1981) 'A new self-report scale of intrinsic versus extrinsic orientation in the classroom: motivational and informational components', *Developmental Psychology*, 17(3): 300–12.

Hattie, J. (2009) *Visible Learning: A Synthesis of Meta-analysis Relating to Achievement*, London: Routledge.

Hattie, J. and Clarke, S. (2019) *Visible Learning: Feedback*, Abingdon, UK: Routledge.

Hattie, J. and Timperley, H. (2007) 'The power of feedback', *Review of Educational Research*, 77(1): 81–112.

Hausman, H. and Kornell, N. (2014) 'Mixing topics while studying does not enhance learning', *Journal of Applied Research in Memory and Cognition*, 3(3): 153–60.

Hayward, L. and Spencer, E. (2010) 'The complexities of change: formative assessment in Scotland', *Curriculum Journal*, 21(2): 161–77.

Hertberg-Davis, H. (2009) 'Myth 7: differentiation in the regular classroom is equivalent to gifted programs and is sufficient: classroom teachers have the time, the skill, and the will to differentiate adequately', *Gifted Child Quarterly*, 53(4): 251–3.

Higgins, S., Katsipataki, M., Kokotsaki, D., Coleman, R., Major, L.E. and Coe, R. (2014) *The Sutton Trust: Education Endowment Foundation Teaching and Learning Toolkit*, London: EEF.

Hill, C. (2020) 'Assessment and feedback: an efficiency model for English', in S. Donarski and T. Bennett (eds), *The ResearchED Guide to Assessment: An Evidence-Informed Guide for Teachers*, Melton, UK: John Catt Educational, pp37–48.

Hogan, R.M. and Kintsch, W. (1971) 'Differential effects of study and test trials on long-term recognition and recall', *Journal of Verbal Learning and Verbal Behavior*, 10: 562–7.

Horvath, J.C. (2019) *Stop Talking, Start Influencing: 12 Insights from Brain Science to Make Your Message Stick*, Gosford: Exisle Publishing.

Howard-Jones, P.A. (2014) 'Evolutionary perspectives on mind, brain and education', *Mind, Brain, and Education*, 8(1): 21–33.

Jones, K. (2019) *Retrieval Practice: Research and Resources for Every Classroom*, Melton, UK: John Catt Educational.

Karably, K. and Zabrucky, K. (2009) 'Children's metamemory: a review of the literature and implications for the classroom', *International Electronic Journal of Elementary Education*, 2(1), available at: http://www.iejee.com/index/makale/19/childrens-metamemory-a-review-of-the-literature-andimplications-for-the-classroom#

Karpicke, J.D. (2017) 'Retrieval-based learning: a decade of progress', in J.T. Wixted (ed.), *Cognitive Psychology of Memory, Vol. 2 of Learning and Memory: A Comprehensive Reference* (J.H. Byrne, Series ed.), Oxford: Academic Press, pp487–514.

Kellard, K., Costello, M., Godfrey, D., Griffiths, E. and Rees, C. (2008) *Evaluation of the Developing Thinking and Assessment for Learning Development Programme*, Cardiff: Welsh Assembly.

King, R. and McInerney, D. (2016) 'Do goals lead to outcomes or can it be the other way around? Causal ordering of mastery goals, metacognitive strategies, and achievement', *British Journal of Educational Psychology*, 86(3): 296–312.

Kirschner, P.A., Sweller, J. and Clark, R.E. (2006) 'Why minimal guidance during instruction does not work: an analysis of the failure of constructivist, discovery, problem-based, experiential, and enquiry-based teaching', *Educational Psychologist*, 41(2): 75–86.

Kirton, A., Hallam, S., Peffers, J., Robertson, P. and Stobart, G. (2007) 'Revolution, evolution or a Trojan horse? Piloting assessment for learning in some Scottish secondary schools', *British Educational Research Journal*, 33(4): 605–27.

Kolić-Vehovec, S. and Bajšanski, I. (2006) 'Metacognitive strategies and reading comprehension in elementary-school students', *European Journal of Psychology of Education*, 21(4): 439–51, available at: https://doi.org/10.1007/BF03173513

Kornell, N. and Bjork, R.A. (2008) 'Learning concepts and categories: is spacing the "enemy of induction"?' *Psychological Science*, 19(6): 585–92, available at: doi: 10.1111/j.1467-9280.2008.02127.x

Larkin, M. (2002) *Using Scaffolded Instruction to Optimize Learning*, Arlington, VA: ERIC Clearinghouse on Disabilities and Gifted Education.

Lemov, D. and Badillo, E. (2020) 'On writing a knowledge-driven English curriculum', in C. Sealy and T. Bennett (eds), *The ResearchED Guide to the Curriculum: An Evidence-Informed Guide for Teachers*, Woodbridge: John Catt Educational, pp85–94.

Leutwyler, B. and Maag Merki, K. (2009) 'School effects on students' self-regulated learning', *Journal for Educational Research Online*, 1: 197–223.

Lovell, O. (2020) *Sweller's Cognitive Load Theory in Action*, Melton, UK: John Catt Educational.

Lucas, T. and Villegas, A.M. (2013) 'Preparing linguistically responsive teachers: laying the foundations in preservice teacher education', *Theory into Practice*, 52: 98–109.

MacPhail, A. and Halbert, J. (2010) '"We had to do intelligent thinking during recent PE": students' and teachers' experiences of assessment for learning in post-secondary physical education', *Assessment in Education: Principles, Policy and Practice*, 17(1): 23–39.

Maguire, E.A., Woollett, K. and Spiers, H.J. (2006) 'London taxi drivers and bus drivers: a structural MRI and neuropsychological analysis', *Hippocampus*, 16(12): 1091–101.

Matusz, P.J., Broadbent, H., Ferrari, J., Forrest, B., Merkley, R. and Scerif, G. (2015) 'Multimodal distraction: insights from children's limited attention', *Cognition*, 136: 156–65.

McKinney, J.D., Mason, J., Perkerson, K. and Clifford, M. (1975) 'Relationship between classroom behaviour and academic achievement', *Journal of Educational Psychology*, 67: 198–203.

McLeod, S. (2013) 'Stages of memory: encoding storage and retrieval', *Simply Psychology*, available at: www.simplypsychology.org/memory.html

Meyer, I.H. (2003) 'Prejudice, social stress, and mental health in lesbian, gay and bisexual populations: conceptual issues and research evidence', *Psychological Bulletin*, 129: 674–97.

Miller, G. (1956) 'The magical number seven, plus or minus two: some limits on our capacity for processing information', *The Psychological Review*, 63(2): 81–97.

Moore, D.S. (2015) *The Developing Genome: An introduction to Behavioral Epigenetics*, New York: Oxford University Press.

Moreno, R. (2004) 'Decreasing cognitive load in novice students: effects of explanatory versus corrective feedback in discovery-based multimedia', *Instructional Science*, 32: 99–113.

Morris, I. (2009) *Teaching Happiness and Well-being in Schools: Learning to Ride Elephants*, London: Continuum International Publishing Group.

Moyles, J. and Suschitzky, W. (1997) 'The employment and deployment of classroom support staff: head teachers' perspectives', *Research in Education*, 58(1): 21–34.

Muijs, D. and Bokhove, C. (2020) *Metacognition and Self-Regulation: Evidence Review*, London: Education Endowment Foundation, available at: https://educationendowmentfoundation.org.uk/public/files/Metacognition_and_self-regulation_review.pdf

Nadolski, R.J., Kirschner, P.A. and van Merriënboer, J.J.G. (2005) 'Optimising the number of steps in learning tasks for complex skills', *British Journal of Educational Psychology*, 75: 223–37.

National Education Union (NEU) (2021) 'Turning the page on poverty: a practical guide for education staff to help tackle poverty and the cost of the school day', London: NEU.

Needham, T. (2019) 'Teaching through examples', in A. Boxer and T. Bennett (eds), *The ResearchED Guide to Explicit and Direct Instruction*, Melton, UK: John Catt Educational, pp37–53.

Nieto, S. (2000) 'Placing equity front and center: some thoughts on transforming teacher education for a new century', *Journal of Teacher Education* 51: 180–7.

Oakes, L.M., Kannass, K.N. and Shaddy, D.J. (2002) 'Developmental changes in endogenous control of attention: the role of target familiarity on infants' distraction latency', *Child Development*, 73: 1644–55.

Odell, F. (2020) 'Assessment and feedback as part of a progression model', in S. Donarski and T. Bennett (eds), *The ResearchED Guide to Assessment: An Evidence-Informed Guide for Teachers*, Melton, UK: John Catt Educational, pp123–36.

Office for Standards in Education (Ofsted) (2002) *The Curriculum in Successful Primary Schools*, available at: http://dera.ioe.ac.uk/4564/1/Curriculum%20in%20successful%20primary%20 schools%20%28The%29%20%28PDF%20format%29.pdf

Office for Standards in Education (Ofsted) (2019) *Guidance: Education Inspection Framework*, available at: https://www.gov.uk/government/publications/education-inspection-frame-work/education-inspection-framework

Office for Standards in Education (Ofsted) (2021) *Guidance: School Inspection Handbook*, available at: https://www.gov.uk/government/publications/school-inspection-handbook-eif/school-inspection-handbook

Ollerton, M. (2001) 'Inclusion, learning and teaching mathematics: beliefs and values', in P. Gates (ed.), *Issues in Mathematics Teaching*, London: RoutledgeFalmer.

Paas, F., Renkl, A. and Sweller, J. (2003) 'Cognitive load theory: instructional implications of the interaction between information structures and cognitive architecture', *Instructional Science*, 32(1/2): 1–8.

Pashler, H., McDaniel, M., Rohrer, D. and Bjork, R. (2009) 'Learning styles: concepts and evidence', *Psychological Science in the Public Interest*, 9(3): 105–19.

Pastötter, B. and Bäuml, K.-H.T. (2019) 'Testing enhances subsequent learning in older adults', *Psychology and Aging*, 34: 242–50.

Peterson, L.R. and Peterson, M.J. (1959) 'Short-term retention of individual verbal items', *Journal of Experimental Psychology*, 58: 193–8.

Polesel, J., Rice, S. and Dulfer, N. (2014) 'The impact of high-stakes testing on curriculum and pedagogy: a teacher perspective from Australia', *Journal of Education Policy*, 29(5): 640–57.

Powley, R. (2020) 'In pursuit of the powerful: knowledge, knowers and knowing', in S. Donarski and T. Bennett (eds), *The ResearchED Guide to Assessment: An Evidence-Informed Guide for Teachers*, Melton, UK: John Catt Educational, pp59–72.

Radford, J., Blatchford, P. and Webster, R. (2011) 'Opening up and closing down: comparing teacher and TA talk in mathematics lessons', *Learning and Instruction*, 21(5): 625–35.

Rawson, A. and Kintsch, W. (2005) 'Rereading effects depend on time of test', *Journal of Educational Psychology*, 97(1): 70–80.

Reay, D. (2017) *Miseducation: Inequality, Education and the Working-Classes*, Bristol: Policy Press.

Reid, A. (2020) 'Cultural capital, critical theory and curriculum', in C. Sealy (ed.), *The ResearchED Guide to the Curriculum: An Evidence-Informed Guide for Teachers*, Melton, UK: John Catt Educational, pp41–8.

Richland, L.E., Bjork, R.A., Finley, J.R. and Linn, M.C. (2005) 'Linking cognitive science to education: generation and interleaving effects', in B.G. Bara, L. Barsalou and M. Bucciarelli (eds), *Proceedings of the Twenty-Seventh Annual Conference of the Cognitive Science Society*, Mahwah, NJ: Lawrence Erlbaum, 1850–1855.

Riener, C. and Willingham, D. (2010) 'The myth of learning styles', *Change: The Magazine of Higher Learning*, 42: 32–5.

Rizvi, N. (2019) 'Communicating through covertization: constructing cognitive routines', in A. Boxer and T. Bennett (eds), *The ResearchED Guide to Explicit and Direct Instruction*, Melton, UK: John Catt Educational, pp75–85.

Roblyer, M.D. (1996) 'The constructivist/objectivist debate: implications for instructional technology research', *Learning and Leading With Technology*, 24: 12–16.

Roediger, H.L., III, and Karpicke, J.D. (2006) 'Test-enhanced learning: taking memory tests improves long-term retention', *Psychological Science*, 17: 249–55.

Roediger, H.L. III, Putnam, A.L. and Smith, M.A. (2011) 'Ten benefits of testing and their applications to educational practice', in J.P. Mestre and B.H. Ross (eds), *The Psychology of Learning and Motivation: Cognition in Education*, New York: Elsevier Academic Press, pp1–36, available at: https://doi.org/10.1016/B978-0-12-387691-1.00001-6

Roffey, S. (2017) 'Ordinary magic needs ordinary magicians: the power and practice of positive relationships for building youth resilience and wellbeing', *Kognition & Pædagogik*, 103: 38–57.

Rohrer, D., Dedrick, R. and Stershic, S. (2015) 'Interleaved practice improves mathematics learning', *Journal of Educational Psychology*, 107(3): 900–8.

Rosenshine, B. (2010) *Principles of Instruction*, International Academy of Education, UNESCO. Geneva: International Bureau of Education, available at: http://www.ibe.unesco.org/fileadmin/user_upload/Publications/Educational_Practices/EdPractices_21.pdf

Rosenshine, B. (2012) 'Principles of instruction: research based principles that all teachers should know', *American Educator*, Spring 2012, available at: http://www.aft.org/pdfs/americaneducator/spring2012/Rosenshine.pdf

Rubie-Davies, C., Blatchford, P., Webster, R., Koutsoubou, M. and Bassett, P. (2010) 'Enhancing student learning? A comparison of teacher and teaching assistant interaction with pupils', *School Effectiveness and School Improvement*, 21(4): 429–49.

Ryan, R.M. and Deci, E.L. (2000) 'Self-determination theory and the facilitation of intrinsic motivation, social development and well-being', *American Psychologist*, 55(91): pp68–78.

Scheerens, J. and Bosker, R. (1997) *The Foundations of Educational Effectiveness*, Oxford: Pergamon.

Schunk, D.H., Hanson, A.R. and Cox, P.D. (1987) 'Peer-model attributes and students' achievement behaviors', *Journal of Educational Psychology*, 79: 54–61.

Sealy, C. (2019) 'Memorable experiences are the best way to help children remember things', in C. Barton and T. Bennett (eds), *The ResearchED guide to Education Myths: An Evidence-Informed Guide for Teachers*, Melton, UK: John Catt Educational, pp29–40.

Sealy, C. (2020) 'Introduction', in C. Sealy and T. Bennett (eds), *The ResearchED Guide to the Curriculum: An Evidence-Informed Guide for Teachers*, Melton, UK: John Catt Educational, pp13–18.

Seidel, T. and Shavelson, R.J. (2007) 'Teaching effectiveness research in the past decade: the role of theory and research design in disentangling meta-analysis results', *Review of Educational Research*, 77(4): 454–99.

Sharples, J., Blatchford, P. and Webster, R. (2016) 'Making best use of teaching assistants', London: Education Endowment Foundation.

Sharples, J., Webster, R. and Blatchford, P. (2015) 'Making best use of teaching assistants – guidance report', London: Education Endowment Foundation.

Sherrington, T. (2017) *The Learning Rainforest: Great Teaching in Great Classrooms*, Melton, UK: John Catt Educational.

Sherrington, T. (2019a) 'Teacher-led instruction and student-centred learning are opposites', in C. Barton and T. Bennett (eds), *The ResearchED guide to Education Myths: An Evidence-Informed Guide for Teachers*, Melton, UK: John Catt Educational, pp71–82.

Sherrington, T. (2019b) *Rosenshine's Principles in Action*, Melton, UK: John Catt Educational.

Sherrington, T. (2020) 'Authentic assessment', in S. Donarski and T. Bennett (eds), *The ResearchED Guide to Assessment: An Evidence-Informed Guide for Teachers*, Melton, UK: John Catt Educational, pp149–65.

Simons, J. and Porter, N. (eds) (2015) *Knowledge and the Curriculum*, London: Policy Exchange.

Slavich, G.M. and Cole, S.W. (2013) 'The emerging field of human social genomics', *Clinical Psychological Science*, 1(3): 331–48.

Slavin, R.E. (1987) 'Ability grouping and student achievement in elementary schools: a best-evidence synthesis', *Review of Educational Research*, 57(3): 293–336.

Slavin, R.E. (1990) 'Achievement effects of ability grouping in secondary schools: a best-evidence synthesis', *Review of Educational Research*, 60: 471–99.

Sleeter, C.E. (2011) 'An agenda to strengthen culturally responsive pedagogy', *English Teaching: Practice and Critique*, 10(2): 7–23.

Spielman, A. (2019) [Keynote speech] *The Wonder Years' Curriculum Conference*, Pimlico Academy, London, 26 January.

Steele, A., Karmiloff-Smith, A., Cornish, K. and Scerif, G. (2012) 'The multiple subfunctions of attention: differential developmental gateways to literacy and numeracy', *Child Development*, 83: 2028–41.

Sternberg, R. (2005) 'Intelligence, competence, and expertise', in A. Elliot and C.S. Dweck (eds), *The Handbook of Competence and Motivation*, New York: Guilford Press, 15–30.

Stiggins, R. and Arter, J. (2002) 'Assessment for learning: international perspectives', Proceedings of an international conference, Chester, UK, 18 September 2001, Portland, OR: Assessment Training Inst. Inc.

Stockard, J., Wood, T.W., Coughlin, C. and Rasplica Khoury, C. (2018) 'The effectiveness of direct instruction curricula: a meta-analysis of a half century of research', *Review of Educational Research*, 88(4): 479–507, available at: doi: 10.3102/0034654317751919

Sweller, J., Ayres, P. and Kalyuga, S. (2011) *Cognitive Load Theory: Volume 1*, New York: Springer.

Taylor, S. (2017) 'Contested knowledge: a critical review of the concept of differentiation in teaching and learning', *Warwick Journal of Education – Transforming Teaching*, 1: 55–68.

Terman, L.M. and Oden, M.H. (1947) *The Gifted Child Grows Up: Twenty-Five Years' Follow-Up of a Superior Group*, Oxford, UK: Stanford University Press.

Terwel, J. (2005) 'Curriculum differentiation: multiple perspectives and developments in education', *Journal of Curriculum Studies*, 37(6): 653–70.

Tomlinson, C.A. (2000) 'Differentiation of instruction in the elementary grades', *ERIC Digest*, Syracuse, NY: Office of Educational Research and Improvement (OERI).

Torrance, H. and Pryor, J. (2001) 'Developing formative assessment in the classroom: using action research to explore and modify theory', *British Educational Research Journal*, 27(5): 615–31.

Turner, S. (2019) 'Spirals, strands and revisiting: importance of review and making links in curricular design', in A. Boxer and T. Bennett (eds), *The ResearchED Guide to Explicit and Direct Instruction*, Melton, UK: John Catt Educational, pp131–7.

Veenman, M.V.J., Van Hout-Wolters, B.H.A.M. and Afflerbach, P. (2006) 'Metacognition and learning: conceptual and methodological considerations', *Metacognition Learning*, 1: 3–14, available at: https://doi.org/10.1007/s11409-006-6893-0

Vygotsky, L.S. (1978) *Mind in Society: The Development of Higher Psychological Processes*. Cambridge, MA: Harvard University Press.

Webb, M. and Jones, J. (2009) 'Exploring tensions in developing assessment for learning', *Assessment in Education*, 16(2): 165–84.

Wheelahan, L. (2009) 'The problem with CBT (and why constructivism makes things worse)', *Journal of Education and Work*, 22(3): 227–42.

Wiliam, D. (2012) 'Are there "good" schools and "bad" schools?', in P.S. Adey and J. Dillon (eds), *Bad Education: Debunking Myths in Education*, Maidenhead: Open University Press, pp3–15.

Wiliam, D. (2018) *Creating the Schools Our Children Need: Why What We're Doing Now Won't Help Much (And What We Can Do Instead)*, West Palm Beach, FL: Learning Sciences International.

Wiliam, D. (2020) 'How to think about assessment', in S. Donarski and T. Bennett (eds), *The ResearchED Guide to Assessment: An Evidence-Informed Guide for Teachers*, Melton, UK: John Catt Educational, pp21–36.

Willingham, D.T. (2009) *Why Don't Students Like School? A Cognitive Scientist Answers Questions about How the Mind Works and What It Means for the Classroom*, Hoboken, NJ: John Wiley & Sons.

Young, M. (2008) 'From constructivism to realism in the sociology of the curriculum', *Review of Research in Education*, 32: 1–32.

Young, M. (2013) 'Powerful knowledge: an analytically useful concept or just a "sexy sounding term"? A response to John Beck's "Powerful knowledge, esoteric knowledge, curriculum knowledge"', *Cambridge Journal of Education*, 43: 195–8.

Young, M. (2014) 'Powerful knowledge as a curriculum principle', in M. Young and D. Lambert, with C. Roberts and M. Roberts (eds), *Knowledge and the Future School: Curriculum and Social Justice*, London: Bloomsbury Academic, pp65–88.

Young, M. (2020) 'From powerful knowledge to the powers of knowledge', in C. Sealy and T. Bennett (eds), *The ResearchED Guide to the Curriculum: An Evidence-Informed Guide for Teachers*, Melton, UK: John Catt Educational, pp19–30.

Young, M. and Lambert, D., with C. Roberts and M. Roberts (2014) *Knowledge and the Future School: Curriculum and Social Justice*, London: Bloomsbury Academic.

Zimmerman, B. (2000) 'Self-efficacy: an essential motive to learn', *Contemporary Educational Psychology*, 25(1): 82–91.

Zimmerman, B.J. (2010) 'Becoming a self-regulated learner: an overview', *Theory into Practice*, 41(2): 64–70.

iNDEX

Locators in *italics* refer to figures and those in **bold** to tables.

.